NICOLE KIDMAN

Also by Tim Ewbank and Stafford Hildred

Roy Keane: Captain Fantastic
David Jason: The Biography
Russell Crowe
Julie Christie
Joanna Lumley

NICOLE KIDMAN

The Biography

TIM EWBANK AND
STAFFORD HILDRED

headline

First published in 2002
by HEADLINE BOOK PUBLISHING

10 9 8 7 6 5 4 3 2 1

ISBN 0 7553 1107 8 (Hardback)
ISBN 0 7553 1167 1 (Trade paperback)

Typeset in Weiss by
Letterpart Limited, Reigate, Surrey

Printed and bound in Great Britain by
Mackays of Chatham plc, Chatham, Kent

HEADLINE BOOK PUBLISHING
A division of Hodder Headline
338 Euston Road
LONDON NW1 3BH

www.headline.co.uk
www.hodderheadline.com

Tim: To my daughter Emma Poppie

Stafford: To my wife Janet, my daughters Claire and Rebecca, and my mother Rosemary

✳ CONTENTS ✳

✳ ACKNOWLEDGEMENTS ✳

The authors wish to thank for their help with this book, and for their support, encouragement and inspiration: Roy and Liz Addison, Ahmed Ali, Jason Ashby, Australian Film Institute, John and Tyna Airey, Harry Baker, Ruth Berry, Cindy Blanchflower, Paul Bradley, John and Pippa Burmester, Mel and Ruth Chapman, Michelle Clark, Charmian Cowie, Roger Davis, John and Wendy Dickinson, Ian Dowell, Alan Durrant, Kenneth Easthough, Jane Ennis, Kamilla Escombe, Joy Ewbank, Oliver Ewbank, Carole Anne Ferris, Peter and Janet Garner, Dan Giblin, Donna Giblin, Rod and Joy Gilchrist, Betty Grant, Richard Hall, Phillip and Ann Hammond, Jodie Hazell, Ingrid Holtz, Kay Hurley, Clive Jackson, Fergus Kelly, Barry Kernon, Simon Kinnersley, Robert Kirby, David Knight, Frank and Hazel Langan, Moira Marr, Bryan Marshall, Fraser Massey, Sandra McClain, Rhiannon McCormack, Aysen Mustafa of the AFI Library and Research Services, Yvonne and Richard Partridge, Dimiti Perry, Keith Richmond, Rachel Sharp, Ampy Smith, Peter, Vivienne and Ben Sullivan, David Thompson, Rochelle Tosland, Gordon Webb.

Special thanks to Qantas for their care, comfort and courtesy, and to all at Sullivans Hotel, 21 Oxford Street, Paddington, Sydney, for such a pleasant and enjoyable stay during our research. And a big thank you to Celia Kent, Juliana Lessa and all at Headline for their encouragement and cooperation.

✶

CHAPTER 1

Who's That Girl?

'It was terrifically embarrassing to learn that I was a couple of inches taller'
— NICOLE KIDMAN ON HER FIRST
MEETING WITH TOM CRUISE

Nicole Kidman was feeling decidedly out of sorts. She was fighting a worsening cold, she was tired, and she was suffering the effects of a long, uncomfortable and restless flight across the Pacific from Japan to California. As her plane neared Los Angeles international airport, she fastened her seat-belt in preparation for the descent through the cloud of smog which perpetually hangs over the City of Angels and tried to clear her head and gather her thoughts.

Nicole had just spent an arduous few days promoting an Australian movie called *Dead Calm* at a film festival in Japan. Now she was flying into Los Angeles to keep an appointment with Hollywood superstar Tom Cruise who, by virtue of the thrilling action movie *Top Gun* in which he played a fighter pilot with a mind of his own, was just about the hottest male movie star in the world at the time. He was also an international heart-throb, an icon whose handsome features stared down from posters on the bedroom walls of teenagers all over the world.

Nicole had at first been incredulous when she had picked up the telephone in Australia to hear from her agent: 'Tom Cruise is interested in working with you.' As a movie actress she was still a fledgling, and her instant reaction was to scoff 'Oh sure!' Nicole had heard those sorts of rumours many times before. Believing it to be some kind of unfortunate joke, she took some persuading of the reality of it. But it was true. Nicole had left a deep impression upon Tom when he had seen her in *Dead Calm*.

Now she was one day away from meeting the heart-throb actor himself and she was understandably starting to feel nervous at the prospect. Raised from an early age to be independent and to stand up for herself, Nicole was not going to be fazed by meeting an actor of the calibre and celebrity of Cruise. Or so she thought. But she was in awe of him. She had seen almost every film he had made and he was much more than a teen idol. Nicole felt he was a very special actor.

For her own acting career, there was a very great deal riding on the meeting. Tom, whose standing in Hollywood was such that he had a say when it came to casting the movies he starred in, was linking up once more with the hugely successful blockbuster *Top Gun* producers Jerry Bruckheimer and Don Simpson. They were combining to make a new big-budget Hollywood movie provisionally entitled *Daytona* about a stock-car racing driver. Hollywood insiders referred to it as 'Top Car'. Following Tom Cruise's avowed intention to work with Nicole, there was talk of a possible role in the movie for her and she was in Los Angeles to audition for it.

Tom and fellow actor Emilio Estevez, a close friend who had been Tom's best man at his wedding to actress Mimi Rogers, had been to see *Dead Calm* together one night in Los Angeles at a private screening. The word was out in Hollywood that *Dead Calm* was a thrilling movie, a chilling tale in the Alfred Hitchcock mould about a wife on an idyllic sailing cruise with her husband who is left battling for her life when a madman takes control of the boat and leaves the husband stranded on another vessel which is sinking fast. The word was also out that the movie had unearthed a very special talent, an actress of striking beauty from Australia by the name of Nicole Kidman – till then a total unknown in Hollywood.

During the screening, Tom Cruise leaned across to Estevez and whispered: 'Who is that girl?' Estevez had no idea. 'I don't know. I've never heard of her,' he replied. By the time the credits were rolling, Cruise had made up his mind that the actress in the leading role was not only stunning, sexy and different, but showed a rare acting ability and he was going to work with her.

Cruise wasted no time in urging the *Daytona* scriptwriter, Robert Towne, also to go and see *Dead Calm*. Like Cruise, Towne emerged from the screening enthusing over the Australian actress with the distinctive red ringlets and agreed with the actor that a role for her could be written into their movie. And so it was that Nicole flew into Los Angeles for a meeting that was to turn her life upside down both personally and professionally in a way that she cannot possibly have imagined.

The night before the audition, a script arrived for Nicole at the hotel room she had been booked into. Despite her cold, she spent time going over and over it until jet-lag finally overwhelmed her. Next morning, Nicole was still feeling not a little disoriented as she set off for the audition at the *Daytona* production office. Arriving with time to spare, she was astonished to find that she was the sole actress expected for the audition. She had imagined that she would be just one of dozens of actresses in line for the role of Tom Cruise's love interest in *Daytona*. She ran her eyes over the script again and then, at the appointed hour, took a deep breath and walked into the conference room to find herself confronted by six men, a studio executive and the five key team members of the *Daytona* project. Six pairs of male eyes scrutinised Nicole's entrance as she stepped forward to be introduced to them all one by one – producers Jerry Bruckheimer and Don Simpson, writer Robert Towne, director Tony Scott, a studio executive, and the handsome megastar himself, Tom Cruise.

Nicole could hardly have come face to face with a more powerful array of Hollywood movie heavyweights than if she had hand-picked them herself. Bruckheimer and Simpson were a dynamic duo with an extraordinary track record when it came to making hit movies. They had first combined in 1983 on *Flashdance*, a film about a girl who toiled in a Pittsburgh steel mill by day and let off steam at night by performing wild, improvised dances in a local bar. Despite the lack of an established star, the movie grossed an astonishing $270 million. The duo topped that the following year as producers of the hugely successful *Beverly Hills Cop*, starring Eddie Murphy, which grossed $350 million.

Sitting beside the two producers with the Midas touch was Robert Towne, a top-class scriptwriter whose complex but literate and orderly screenplay had made *Chinatown*, starring

Jack Nicholson as a gumshoe on a murder manhunt, such an outstanding movie. Next to him was British director Tony Scott, whose movie *Top Gun* had become the biggest grossing film of 1986. Not only that, it went on to become the first blockbuster movie to outgross its take at the cinema when it was issued on video. The total gross eventually topped half a billion dollars.

Then there was, of course, Tom Cruise himself, already a movie icon with a string of hits including *Risky Business*, *Top Gun*, *The Color of Money* and *Rain Man*, an international sex symbol and one of Hollywood's most bankable stars. Nicole had heard he had put in an extraordinary performance in a yet to be released movie called *Born on the Fourth of July*, playing a wheelchair-bound Vietnam veteran.

Inwardly Nicole was quaking. Not long out of her teens, she was thoroughly intimidated by facing a battery of such influential Hollywood players. Any film combining their talents could not fail. In turn they each rose to shake hands with her. But if her insides were churning, Nicole didn't outwardly show it. Bruckheimer distinctly remembers noticing her fingers and palm to be unexpectedly warm in his grip. It made an immediate positive impression upon him. In his experience of handshakes at past auditions, the interviewees' palms tended almost without exception to be cold which told him they were suffering from nerves.

When Tom Cruise stood up to proffer his hand in greeting, he fixed Nicole with the gaze of a superstar beloved by his legion of female fans – and it had a doubly profound effect on the actress. 'I shook his hand and thought ooooh!' was Nicole's initial reaction. Tom seemed even more handsome to her in the flesh than she remembered on screen. 'He was like this powerhouse. He sort of filled the room . . . the energy coming out was amazing. He had this firm handshake and he told me: "I wanted to meet you . . . I thought you were great in *Dead Calm*." '

But Nicole could not help but notice that as Tom had risen from his seat and drawn himself up to his full height, she was looking down at him. 'It was terrifically embarrassing to learn that I was a couple of inches taller,' she said. 'It wasn't that he was so short, it's more that I'm so tall – five feet eleven.' In that instant she believed that her chances of winning a role in *Daytona* had evaporated even before she had been given the opportunity to utter a single line of dialogue from the script. 'I knew it simply wouldn't do having the girlfriend tower over the macho race car driver,' she said.

The belief that she was almost certainly pursuing a lost cause went some way to calming Nicole's nerves and, as she took her seat and turned to face the panel assembled in judgement of her, she found herself saying: 'Well, there are certainly a lot of men in the room!' Nobody laughed at her attempt at a joke to break the ice. 'I tried to be very nonchalant about the whole thing. I was relaxed, cracking a joke, a sort of defence mechanism,' Nicole remembers.

Extracting her reading glasses from her handbag, Nicole then picked up the script and began to read at the group's bidding from a couple of test pages after it was explained that they had no real part in mind for her as yet. Suddenly she felt comfortable, no longer tense, and her butterflies disappeared. As she had so often found before with her stage roles, once the curtain was up and she was actually getting on with the business in hand she was no longer nervous.

While she went through her lines, the *Daytona* group stared at her impassively and said not a word. Finally she finished, and there was a momentary silence. Then Nicole looked up with a smile and there was Tom Cruise suddenly breaking into laughter. Nicole laughed too. It was laughter born of the release of tension and they found themselves laughing in unison. She remembers them looking at each other as if to say: 'Isn't this absurd?' When Tom began talking, Nicole noticed he became really intense, articulating a lot with his hands. And his eyes started to sparkle.

The audition ended convivially enough, thought Nicole as she gathered up her belongings and prepared to leave. But not for one moment did she believe she had clinched a role in the movie. 'Nice to meet you, see you around some time,' she said brightly, closing the door behind her and consoling herself that the audition had at least afforded her the chance to visit Los Angeles and meet Tom Cruise. Inside the conference room, Tom Cruise quickly glanced round his colleagues then, with a grin, said simply: 'Wow!' Tom was famously to say much later of the moment he had first seen Nicole: 'My first reaction to her was lust. Then I got to know her and it was trust. Lust and trust, that was it.'

Nicole came away from the meeting with very positive opinions about Tom. 'When I met him I was struck by what a charming and tender man he is,' she later explained. 'There was no affectation that he was important or a star, nor did he expect you to look up to him. He's certainly exceptional looking – he's got a fantastic face and the cutest smile in the world. No wonder he's every woman's dream.'

The following morning Nicole received a telephone call to say that the part, still not yet written, was hers. The *Daytona* story would be altered to include her. 'But what about my height?' she asked anxiously. 'It doesn't bother Tom,' came the reply, 'so it doesn't bother us.' That was another mark in Tom's favour to add to the agreeable impression the actor had already made upon her. Nicole liked a man who was not afraid of being seen with a taller woman. She had met many men shorter than her who found it difficult to cope with.

Nicole was at that time learning seven pages of dialogue for another movie she was being considered for and for which she was about to audition. Despite the *Daytona* offer, she sensibly went ahead that day with the second audition and secured that role too. After one year of yearning to work in Hollywood, she now had the offer of two films in a day.

While Nicole weighed up the offers, the *Daytona* team made it clear that they were not going to take no for an answer. She found herself receiving dazzling bouquets of flowers from the *Daytona* quintet, and Jerry Bruckheimer and Tom Cruise began ringing her urging her to come on board. There were promises that her role would not be like that of a Bond girl in the 007 movies. She would not be there just for decoration. Hers would be a role of substance, Nicole was assured. The actress later recalled: 'Tom was saying: "I don't care what it costs, you get on this movie. I don't care what happens, you get on this movie, you have to do this film." It was bizarre.' And very persuasive.

Bizarre or not, it was hard for Nicole not to be swayed by Tom Cruise's cloying enthusiasm and his charm, and soon a very definite role in the film emerged for her. She would play Dr Claire Lewicki, a strong-willed medical intern with whom Tom Cruise's racing driver Cole Trickle falls in love while being treated after an accident on the race track.

Returning to Australia to think things over, Nicole found there was no shortage of advice about her first steps into

Hollywood. Terry Hayes, one of her great mentors in the Australian film industry and a man whose judgement she trusted implicitly, urged her to take the *Daytona* project, which soon came to be renamed *Days of Thunder*, the title under which the movie would eventually be released.

Eventually she decided that the sheer Hollywood weight behind *Days of Thunder* was impossible to ignore. Moreover, the opportunity for an Australian actress to appear in a big American commercial film was so rare. In fact, no one in Hollywood could think of an Australian actress who had made a big impact in American movies apart from Olivia Newton-John in *Grease* and she had come to the screen on the back of a hugely successful singing and recording career. The producers, and Tom Cruise in particular, were delighted when Nicole signed up with them.

After flying back to Los Angeles from Australia, Nicole was driven straight to Paramount studios for a wardrobe fitting. It was ten o'clock at night by the time she was chauffeured through the gates and stepped out into the car park. It was a typical warm, balmy Californian evening and above her a silvery moon seemed to shine down benevolently. All was quiet and she decided to have a brief look round the studio buildings to find her bearings. Then, returning to the car park, she stood silently bathed in the moonlight gazing in awe at the studio lots. She had to pinch herself that she was really there, a young actress about to have a wardrobe fitting for a Paramount film.

Paramount's trademark of snow-capped mountain peak surrounded by a half circle of twenty-four stars had come to represent 'peak achievement' and down the years of its illustrious history Paramount had created some of the world's most dazzling female movie stars, such as Mary Pickford, Gloria Swanson, Myrna Loy, Tallulah Bankhead, Mae West, Claudette

Colbert, Paulette Goddard, Veronica Lake and Hedy Lamarr. It was here that Alfred Hitchcock had directed Grace Kelly in *Rear Window*, that Paramount's legendary movie pioneer Cecil B. DeMille had called 'action' for the first time and gone on to craft some of the great films of his day. It was Paramount who had brought to the screen a seductive German actress by the name of Marlene Dietrich in a sleazy cabaret in which she had so memorably leaned back to flash her magnificent stockinged legs and sung 'Falling in love again . . .' Sophia Loren, Shirley Maclaine, Natalie Wood, Ali MacGraw, Jane Fonda – the list of actresses who had made their mark in movies under the Paramount banner was endless.

'Oh God, this is where they made them. This is where they made the stars,' Nicole remembers saying to herself. She wondered whether Hollywood might work some of that same magic for her because she was dazzled by the place, but she was intimidated and she felt as if she did not belong.

CHAPTER 2

Aloha

'It was about giving us confidence as women to be whatever we wanted to be. The main emphasis was sisterhood because my mother always said it was about helping other women'
— NICOLE KIDMAN ON THE INFLUENCE OF HER FEMINIST MOTHER ON HER UPBRINGING

J ust over 100 years before proud parents Antony and Janelle Kidman celebrated the birth of their first child Nicole in Hawaii, a young man struck out to make his fortune in Adelaide, South Australia. A century before baby Nicole was delighting her mother and father on the exotic holiday islands on the other side of the world, her most famous ancestor was founding a fortune from the most unlikely starting point.

Sidney Kidman was the fifth son of an English farmer who arrived in Australia with little more than dreams. Sadly Kidman senior was still virtually penniless when he died at thirty-nine leaving five sons and a pregnant wife. Sidney was just six months old when his father died. His mother went from bad to worse. She married a farmhand who turned out to be a drunkard – much better at spending money than he was at earning it.

It was a tough start for any youngster but it made Sidney determined to leave home to fend for himself as soon as he was able to. He was just thirteen years old when he carefully waited until his uncaring family were fast asleep before running away from his unhappy home. He left astride his only friend in the world, a one-eyed horse. He had bought his faithful steed with money he had slowly managed to save from his long hours working in the local saleyards. He had just five shillings in his pocket but he was equipped with a quick mind and a rat-like cunning. By the time he died in 1935, Sir Sidney Kidman owned a chunk of Australia that was larger than Great Britain and had established the Kidman name as a by-word for decency and straight dealing, as well as for wealth and success.

Sidney's first job was working as a bushman, roaming the hard and unforgiving country taking care of his stock. As the junior of the team he was ordered to share his sleeping area with an Aboriginal youth called Billy. Many of the men scorned the Aborigines but not Sidney. He was never exactly a God-fearing man but he believed all men were equal. Sidney and Billy became mates. Treating people decently was to pay off for Sidney, because Billy taught him tracking and other Aboriginal bush skills. This gave him a vital edge when he started to run his own cattle. Few people could beat Kidman for knowing where to move his cattle to in droughts.

He became a drover and stock trader before eventually buying the Owen Springs station in the Northern Territory. Before long, he had a chain of stations from the Gulf of Carpentaria in the north down to South Australia, and from

Flinders Ranges to Fitzroy Crossing. He also developed a wide range of other business interests, and made so much money that his old family company is still the biggest landowner in Australia.

Sidney Kidman never moaned about his difficult upbringing, but he learned from his hard times. He never smoked, drank or swore and he was a faithful husband to the hard-working schoolteacher he eventually took to be his wife. 'Family first' was one of his dictums. He believed that a person's strength came from their family and that happiness in the home was to be prized above all else.

Several generations later one of Sidney Kidman's descendants, by the name of Antony Kidman, founded his own family on precisely those principles of hard work, honesty and family loyalty. Antony married Janelle, as the Kidman family story goes, after meeting her on a blind date.

Janelle was nineteen and Antony just a year older when they met, and the young couple soon fell in love. Their relationship was lively, challenging and happy and they had the same warm and open sense of humour. But they followed different religions. Antony was Catholic and Janelle was Protestant and her father at first said he would not be paying the bill for the wedding if there was any talk of his daughter converting. That reservation was quietly dropped later. Antony and Janelle married four years after that first meeting, in the chapel of St Aloysius, Antony's old school, and not too long afterwards Janelle did indeed become a Catholic. In time both their daughters were baptised in the faith as well.

Not long after Antony and Janelle married, they went to live in Honolulu. Some of Sir Sidney's millions would certainly have come in handy in those early days of their marriage but sadly none of the vast wealth or acres of land had passed down to this distant relative. Antony was an ambitious graduate student living on a small stipend at the University of Hawaii, so they were both relieved when Janelle managed to land a part-time job on the campus as a secretary. She had never typed before in her life and had to teach herself at night, well out of sight of her employer. She also quickly signed up for a crash course in shorthand.

Janelle was determined to make a success of the job because the money was very handy to the cash-strapped young couple. They were delighted and relieved when she was taken on full-time. Antony was able to study knowing Janelle was earning a decent salary, and best of all she was working regular hours. It was so different from the nursing she had done back at home in Australia.

It was 20 June 1967 when their first child decided to arrive. A large-limbed baby they named Nicole was born while the Kidmans were working in Hawaii and with the benefit of hindsight the family now consider this was easily the most fortunate place for her to come into the world. Janelle has said she believes that dual Australian–American citizenship is one of the best birthday presents they could have given Nicole. Years later it was to bypass all those awkward visa restrictions and allow her to work unhindered in both Australia and America.

The family moved to Washington for Antony to do post-doctoral studies at the National Institution of Mental Health. The Kidmans spent the next three years in Washington while Antony did breast cancer research on a National Institute of Health grant. Their first daughter can only dimly remember her early American upbringing. 'I have a vague recollection of it being very cold with lots of snow,' says Nicole. 'I remember eating snow and my parents throwing snowballs at each other.'

When she was four Nicole moved back with her parents to their beloved Sydney. She was by all accounts an outstandingly rebellious child. She was confident, had a will of her own and was extremely strong-minded. But this was anything but a conventional family. Both Antony and Janelle believed deeply in free thinking and originality and they encouraged Nicole and her younger sister Antonia to express themselves and nurtured their spirited independence.

One famous Kidman family story recalls the time when Nicole asked for a Barbie doll for Christmas. When her mother, an ardent feminist, flatly refused the request for the sexist toy, the little girl is said to have simply got herself one from a store. There always was a direct, almost anarchic side to the young Nicole Kidman. The relative to whom she related most closely was her father's father: 'a gambler who won and lost fortunes'. But Nicole's theatrical enthusiasm seems to have come from within. Her father did take part in amateur theatricals when a student, but otherwise there is no record of acting ability in the family.

When they returned from their sojourn in the United States, Antony and Janelle settled in the stylish Sydney suburb of Longueville, a comfortable conservative area where leafy avenues of elegant California-style bungalows and houses jostle gently for a view of the water. The Kidmans made their home in affluent, well-kept William Edward Street in an unostentatious two-storey house surrounded by a neatly kept garden. It was at nearby Lane Cove that Nicole went to the local primary school.

Longueville was settled by Europeans at the end of the eighteenth century. Many of the first land grants were made in 1794 to privates and NCOs from the New South Wales Corp by their grateful commanding officer Lieutenant Governor Francis Grose. But most of the men traded their land and the eventual settlers found Longueville to be anything but the sleepy suburb it is today. Most of the area is steep and it was very heavily timbered with poor rocky soil. The settlers were plagued by troublesome Aborigines and natural hazards such as bushfires and poisonous snakes. A historian described Longueville as a country with impenetrable cliffs and forests all along the river with tall grasslands on the ridges and said it was: 'The resort of disreputable people . . . as great a set of ruffians as the colony holds.'

Today it is rather different. The drives of the houses play host mainly to the BMWs and Mercedes of the upper middle class. Tennis courts, golf courses and children's playgrounds are sprinkled between the stylish homes, and living in Longueville, just a fifteen-minute drive from the centre of Sydney, is a definite indication of social status.

Antony and Janelle, though, were much more interested in ideas than in possessions. They wanted a good home for their growing family certainly, but they were always much more inquiring than acquisitive. Nicole's sister, Antonia, had arrived by then and from the start the parents taught both their daughters to ask questions and learn about life. Any religious fervour the family possessed appears to have lapsed with time. They cancelled the girls' booking at the Loreto Catholic School and after Lane Cove Primary School Nicole attended North Sydney Girls' High. Janelle said that she liked the melting pot of the state school system.

Nicole's earliest memories are of a very happy home. Back in nursing, her mother had to work long and awkward hours and Nicole often had to take care of her younger sister. Nicole recalls her father making the girls some very strange sandwiches to take to school. While her classmates with non-working mums were eating beautiful neatly cut sandwiches, she would be embarrassed to tuck into her father's specialities. Nicole said: 'My daddy put a slab of butter on the bread and then yelled "Whaddya want? Peanut butter?" And he wouldn't cut them up or wrap them properly so all the other kids would tease us.'

Nicole's mother was a member of the Women's Electoral Lobby and her father was active in Labour politics in a constituency Labour never won. Nicole and Antonia were endlessly stimulated at home by their positive, passionate parents. 'There was always political discussion at our table,' says Nicole. 'We had a sit-down dinner every night and politics was the sort of thing to discuss.' The girls would be encouraged to understand both standpoints of any argument and once they had developed their views they would be expected to defend them. That was fine at home but when Antony and Janelle took their beliefs on to the streets it was sometimes uncomfortable for the girls.

When she was a teenager, the outspoken liberal opinions of her parents did sometimes embarrass Nicole. The doomed duty of handing out Labour Party how-to-vote cards on polling day is not one of her happier childhood memories. 'I would have a cap on hiding my face in case any of the kids saw me,' she said. She also supported her mother in campaigning for the Australian women's movement: 'I would hand out pamphlets on the streets with her and be scoffed at. At the time I was shockingly embarrassed my mother was like this.'

Nicole believes this early experience in standing up and being counted for your beliefs stands her in good stead. She is certainly her mother's daughter: 'I have never been intimidated by a man. My father was gentle but strong, and a good role model. So I have always liked men. I was not brought up to hate them. But I never thought that because I was a woman I wouldn't be able to achieve something. I went to an all-girls school and the attitude there was, "You're a woman, so go for it." '

It was certainly never a boring household. Nicole Kidman grew up in a family who yelled a lot. People would openly and noisily lose their tempers in their house, things would be thrown, and then an hour later they would all sit around and have a laugh together over their differences. Her parents were models of reality in other ways. In one early interview Nicole said: 'They came close to divorce many times. So yelling and screaming that it is all over . . . none of that scares me. My mother moved out once, I think for a couple of weeks. So I don't have a lot of fear of people not coming back.'

Ever keen to expand her range of talents, young Nicole learned to play the violin, clarinet and piano. She also wrote angst-ridden prose. An early heroine was Samantha in *Bewitched*, played by Elizabeth Montgomery. Nicole is said to have tried to turn one of her teachers into a donkey in a bid to emulate Samantha. Nicole said: 'When I have my hair straightened a lot of people say that I look like a young Elizabeth Montgomery which I take as a real compliment.'

Nicole always had a strong personality. A friend of her sister Antonia's recalled: 'When I was nine I went to her little sister's birthday party. Nicole bossed us around and made us play games properly.' Yet Nicole was not always so dominant. She remembers how wonderfully well her mother looked after her whenever she was ill: 'As a kid when I was sick she was a goddess, sitting beside the bed, bringing beautiful warm porridge with cream and brown sugar. And she would massage me gently to make me feel better.'

Antony Kidman has written a series of successful self-help books that encourage readers to recognise rather than suppress their emotions and he certainly believes in practising what he preaches. From an early age Nicole read books that were adult and challenging. To this day she is convinced that was a great way to grow up. 'Yeah of course, you're a kid, that's what you do. I read *Lady Chatterley's Lover*. But my mother would bring home films from the school of nursing when we were twelve to show us sex. We would have to sit there and look at everything in detail, everything.'

Antony and Janelle were determined that their daughters would not lack for education. Nicole remembers being taken to modern dance classes, where the dancers were totally naked. She would be sitting next to her father when she was nine or ten and fully grown men would be walking around naked. 'Did your dad say anything about it?' asked one astonished interviewer and Nicole responded: 'He just said to accept it for what it was. And later he might say "Wasn't that artistic and wonderful?" ' It was embarrassing at times, of course, but it helped to build a rock-solid relationship between parents and daughters. They would drive home and talk. Antony believes in communication. He would ask: 'What do you think about that? How do you feel?' Nicole would say: Oh, Dad, shut up.' But as a result of all the years of frankness and openness, Nicole can today call her father at three in the morning and tell him absolutely anything.

Janelle rose in her profession and went on to teach nursing. She had really wanted to be a doctor, but in those days Australia was far behind in the world of women's liberation. Janelle made a success of her career but continued to throw herself energetically into the cause of feminism. 'My mother was a strong feminist and a tough lady and my father always used the phrase when we were growing up: "With love, but firm",' says Nicole. 'Believe me I grew up with all the rules and guidelines and boundaries. My sister and I were only allowed to watch half an hour of television a day!'

Janelle used her nurse's training to teach her two little daughters about sex. 'My mother once said that she wished she had had a boy that she could raise as a feminist male,' said Nicole. Her father encouraged both Nicole and Antonia to keep their bodies fit and their minds open and the sisters would exercise and do push-ups from an early age. Nicole began ballet lessons when she was three. But she remembers being shy as a child and even experiencing a stutter at one stage. Her determination helped her get over it but she remains shy at heart and insisted even years later that she finds it hard to walk into a crowded room on her own.

It was an unusual and often challenging childhood but it worked. There was a healthy lack of sentimentality about Nicole's life. She recalls that when she was a little girl she would get up early and go out fishing with her grandfather. She said: 'I didn't catch big fish, just lots of little ones that covered the bottom of the boat. I would always get very upset about the hooks coming out of the fishes' mouths and cry.' And did that influence her grandfather to throw the creatures back into the water? 'Not really,' she laughed. 'He would say, "Snap out of it. You eat them don't you?" ' Nicole has often said: 'My childhood really grounded me.' But her parents were always protective as well as permissive. Nicole was furious when they refused to consent to her making a parachute jump. 'I tried to convince my parents to let me jump out of the plane. I needed their permission because I was under eighteen. But they wouldn't give it. They have always tried to keep control of me but as I have gotten older and been able to make my own decisions I take my own risks.' A couple of years later she said: 'I still want to jump out of that plane but I have been working so much that I haven't had the time. Besides there is always the chance that I will break a leg and be out of a job.'

When she had her first boyfriend, at fifteen, her parents allowed the fortunate Doug – a surfer and a carpenter – to stay overnight in the family home. Nicole says: 'My parents were pretty good. He was allowed to stay overnight. My mother was scared of young men who drink and drive since they have the highest statistics for road accidents so she much preferred me safe at home. He wasn't in my bed – he had a separate one in my room like when you had a girlfriend to stay. I kept whispering, "Come, get in my bed." '

Growing up was by no means a painless process. As a child Nicole was teased for her height, her freckles and her curly red hair. She was even occasionally bullied. But not for long. Janelle Kidman was determined to protect her daughters and would embarrass Nicole even further by rushing down to school to confront her tormentors. 'But the great thing my mother did,' says Nicole, 'was that she was always on my side.'

Nicole grew very tall very quickly. By puberty she towered over most of the other boys and girls in her class and thought of herself as 'the ugliest person on earth'. At thirteen she was nicknamed 'The Stork' by the boys at school and she was not even happy with her trademark hair: 'It is very long and weird and I hate it. I have even tried to straighten it because I don't like curly hair.' A schoolfriend recalled that Nicole used to wash her hair on a Sunday night in 'this rosewater stuff' and when she came to class on Monday, 'It used to stink the whole room out. It smelled like some sort of toilet freshener.'

Nicole hated being different. 'I hated the unconventional stuff as a kid because you just want to conform. I was embarrassed by it. I was not one of those kids who want to stand out. I was five feet ten when I was eleven years old,' she says. 'But not being normal gives you this strange thing. You have to develop into a personality. And I wanted to go to drama school because I could escape into characters.'

Janelle used to tell Nicole: 'You'll appreciate being taller when you're older.' 'She is a tall woman and of course she was right, but I didn't think so then.' But gradually Nicole grew more at ease with her towering size. It led to paradoxical situations in which her striking good looks ensured she was the first one of her friends to be selected by modelling agencies, while at school she was still the last one to be asked to dance. Nicole remembers with anguish the confidence-draining experience of being North Sydney Girls' High School's most flamboyant wallflower. She would be forced to stand pressing her back to the wall as all her girlfriends were whisked on to the floor. 'I distinctly remember having one boy dragged to me kicking and screaming going, "I don't want to dance with her",' says Nicole. 'I mean, can you imagine?' She laughs about it now but it was clearly devastating at the time.

Inside the family home the mantelpiece groaned with

photographs of the girls growing up. There were none of the more glamorous pictures of later teenage years when the girls both emerged as real beauties. And the house was distinctive for its total lack of ostentation. Friends of the family all say that Antony and Janelle were totally disinterested in appearance and drilled into their daughters not to judge people by what they looked like.

When she was about fourteen, Nicole suddenly transformed into a beautiful young woman. But even after she was being hailed as a beauty, her parents were delighted that she kept up with her old friends who had been chosen because of their personalities rather than their good looks. Before then Nicole was a real tomboy, enjoying all sports and frequently coming home with scraped knees. Janelle's remedy for scraped knees was exactly the same as it was for all difficult moments, a nice cup of tea. She might have been one of Australia's most formidable feminists but her belief in the healing qualities of a cup of tea were totally unshakeable.

At school Nicole was no goody-goody. She tried smoking and sampled alcohol when she was young but she was never a big drinker. One of the teenagers' favourite forbidden tipples at the time was port. 'To this day I can't drink port. I made myself so sick,' she recalls.

'Nicole was always a natural beauty,' remembers a former schoolfriend from North Sydney Girls' High School. 'Even in year eight you would look at Nicole and think, "She is going to be a really beautiful woman one day." She was always pale with lots of freckles and she was taller than all the other girls. She has not really changed. She is just a bit more glamorous now. Nicole was a very intelligent girl, very academic. She was also a nice, down-to-earth type of person. Nicole was very popular among her peers and she was funny. She liked to laugh a lot and she was not at all stuck up.'

In one of her franker moments, Nicole looked back on her time at North Sydney and admitted: 'I was a drama queen. Still am I suppose. In assembly I can remember being so embarrassed to be pointed out and have a teacher shout, "Sarah Bernhardt, please be quiet." I never understood why at the time. I used to think, "My name is Nicole." ' One schoolfriend remembers: 'Nicole was the ringleader of all the drama shows we used to have. Lunchtimes we had to be there on time otherwise we were sacked. We'd have auditions after auditions.' And another recalls Nicole telling her she wanted to be a really good actress, the best in Australia.

The school was a great producer of talent and especially talented women. The atmosphere of the place was, Nicole said: 'OK, you're having a career.' In a nation that hardly led the way in female emancipation: 'That is what the women before us fought for and now I reap the benefits of it and I don't even think how much easier it is for modern generations.'

Nicole's pale and sensitive skin was a liability for a girl growing up in the harsh Australian climate and she spent her childhood covered in suncream and hiding her fair complexion underneath hats. But it did have advantages. Her distinctly un-Australian colouring made her stand out and she was only seventeen when Lord Lichfield discovered her ethereal beauty and photographed her for his list of Australia's ten most beautiful women.

Though not the traditional image of an Aussie beauty – a curvy blonde who could sunbathe all day long – Nicole was quickly in demand from modelling agencies. They liked her long legs, elegantly slim frame and stylish, almost European good looks. She was offered lots of work in her mid-teens and found it a handy way of earning extra pocket money. She could certainly have made it as a model.

One weekend at a modelling assignment an enterprising stylist tinted and revamped the locks that Kidman had been compulsively blow-drying into submission. The following Monday she hit North Sydney High with a head of bright red curls. 'It was the swan thing,' says Rebecca Rigg. 'It just went round the school like wildfire. Nic had found her essence just simply through letting her hair be what it is naturally and that was definitely a turning point for her as a teenager.'

Nicole's debut as a cover girl was on *Dolly* magazine, but she found the work almost stupefyingly boring. She hated the standing around and the obsession with image.

She was more enthusiastic over a brief career one summer with two girlfriends as a singing trio called *Divine Madness*. They sang cover versions of other people's hits with Nicole showing a penchant for Debbie Harry-style numbers. Drinkers at Kinsella's Hotel in Sydney's colourfully cosmopolitan Paddington district roared their approval at the talented teenagers. Nicole was seventeen and she enjoyed the applause, but singing the same songs night after night was certainly not the sort of challenge she was looking for in life and becoming a pop star was never seriously on her agenda. Acting took over again.

CHAPTER 3

First Steps

'She was still a schoolgirl, but she was like a young Katharine Hepburn in that she was so individual in style and looks. She already had incredible charisma and real star quality.'
– SYDNEY PRODUCER – DIRECTOR PETER WILLIAMS

Nicole Kidman was always going to be an actress. For as long ago as she can remember she loved dressing up. It was one of the pleasures she shared with her mother. 'My mum used to always take me to the flea markets because she loves vintage clothes, and she would always dress us in vintage clothing,' says Nicole. 'We would look like these weird old-fashioned children walking around in dresses that were from the twenties. But now of course being my mother's daughter I have a passion for that.'

Nicole grew up loving *The Wizard of Oz* and pantomimes. Nicole recalls: 'At the age of four I was taken to see pantomimes. I loved the sound of everyone in a room together, laughing or calling out. The audience participation enthralled me.' Janelle also took both Nicole and Antonia to see opera and hear classical music when they were very young. It was all part of the learning experience.

She was still a little girl when she became hooked on acting when she played the innkeeper's daughter in the school nativity play. 'I only had two lines but I knew everyone else's lines as well,' laughs Nicole. 'My mother said I was really good and I suppose that was where it all started.' The following year Nicole was just six when she upstaged baby Jesus in another nativity play, playing a sheep. When they were casting the nativity play Nicole decided she wanted to play Mary. She was not at all happy when she missed out on her first leading role and firmly declined the consolation part of villager, deciding to play a sheep instead. 'I made her a costume out of a woolly car seat,' her mother smiles, 'and when Mary came on stage on the big night she was followed by the sheep who proceeded to lie at her feet and bleat through the entire performance.' Nicole laughed years later: 'When Mary was rocking the baby Jesus I went baa, baa, baa and of course everyone went hysterical. This stupid kid trying to upstage Jesus as a sheep. But I got a laugh and I thought, hey this is fun.' Nicole cheerfully admits she was one of those 'awful kids who said everyone's lines'.

Her parents were always fully aware of Nicole's acting ambitions. Antony said: 'Nicole wanted to be an actor almost as long as I can remember.' Janelle recalled the endless run of dramatic productions their older daughter would organise. Janelle smiled as she recalled: 'Invitations would be issued, neighbourhood children would be cashiered into roles, Nicole would be the star, the producer, the director of course and she would be very upset if anyone deviated from her instructions.

But then she has always been like that. She is a bossy boots.'

Nicole always had a wild imagination. At Lane Cove Primary School she pretended she was a witch for two years and was convincing enough to have most of her classmates believing it. She followed that by bringing the house down as the sheep who would not keep quiet.

In her early teens Nicole's first scripted speaking part was in Frank Wedekind's *Spring Awakening*. The first words she uttered on stage were 'Beat me, harder! Harder! Harder!' *Spring Awakening* was an adult piece about sexual repression in the late 1800s. 'I had my first kiss on stage,' she recalls with a chuckle. At the time Nicole's parents were away on holiday and she was being looked after by her grandmother who 'really liked it'.

Even at junior school she knew she loved being on stage. Being tall was embarrassing and miserable but also character building. Having an outstanding difference between you and your peers means 'You have to develop other strengths.' In Nicole's case this meant creating fantasy worlds, inventing characters and building worlds in her mind. That led naturally to a love of acting which she has never lost. If you ask her if she was always confident about her acting abilities she says it is not a matter of confidence at all. She just knew it was what she was going to do with her life: 'I was just always determined that I was going to see it through and that I would be able to accept rejection and not let it leave me incapable of operating or going for another audition.'

She enrolled in drama school at Sydney's Phillip Street Theatre when she was just ten years old: 'I just had this incredible affinity for getting up on stage. Becoming a movie star didn't really enter into it then. When I wasn't in shows I would be a runner for the kids who were. I would get really excited – I just used to get the tingles.'

Nicole began to spend weekends indoors at the small but fashionable theatre. She helped the stage manager and did odd jobs. 'I just loved it. I absolutely loved it. Each weekend I would go to the theatre. I used to just lock myself in there for the whole weekend. I thought it was fantastic. I would be teased a lot though because I would be going off to the theatre instead of going to the beach with all the other boys and girls. I felt like an outsider because of that. But it is character building not to be a pretty child. You can't rely on getting on through your looks so you have to develop real talents.'

Influential Sydney producer–director Peter Williams was instantly impressed at Phillip Street by Nicole's dedication to her craft. She was always on time. She drove herself hard on every role and was always eager to learn. Williams said: 'From the moment Nicole walked into my office at the Phillip Street Theatre to sign up for drama classes she had the manner and attitude of a professional actress. She was still a schoolgirl but she was like a young Katharine Hepburn in that she was so individual in style and looks. She already had incredible charisma and real star quality. I mean she was never a great actress but she was extraordinary in whatever she did. She had that certain something. And she was quite clearly dedicated to her own crusade, which was to become a star.'

Nicole's hard work at Phillip Street for the repertory company called Australian Theatre for Young People soon got her noticed. Tasks were allocated cyclically: actor for one production, stage manager for another, costume designer for a third. The Australian Theatre for Young People, she said, was her entire social life. Her first professional performance came at thirteen as Sylvia in *The Women*. She played the princess in *Sweet*

Bird of Youth and then director Paul Barron chose her to appear in his warm-hearted Australian film *Bush Christmas*, the story of a poor Australian family desperately struggling to make ends meet in the outback by putting all their hopes on their prized racehorse Prince. Working in a real film galvanised young Nicole into growing up fast. She said: 'I couldn't be the kid and I suddenly had to operate in an adult world with adult rules and that is what I did.' She was delighted to get the role but 'I thought filming was boring when I did *Bush Christmas*. I was a fourteen-year-old kid living away from home being treated like an adult. I was having a good time and I was blown away with that.'

Nicole made many television appearances when she was still at school, including one playing a glue-sniffing schoolgirl in two episodes of *A Country Practice*. But mainly she played roles much older than her real age and joked that by the age of fifteen she was known locally for 'playing older sexually frustrated women'.

She has always been extremely single-minded about her work. At fifteen Nicole decided exactly how she was going to live her life: 'No drugs or crazy partying all the time. I was not going to run off the rails, if I was going to make it as an actress then I had to have a disciplined lifestyle. Either give a hundred per cent or don't bother at all. But I was never cast in any of the school plays. And when I tried to get the role of Annie I put on my flattest shoes for the audition, pulled my hair down flat, walked with a stoop and I still didn't get a call back. I was too tall again. There were times when I didn't think I could take any more of that sort of rejection, but I wanted to prove people wrong, it was the greatest motivation of all. I am tough on the outside – you have to be – but I am soft on the inside. You mustn't let it all get to you. I am just like a chocolate in fact, one of those with a hard exterior and a soft centre.'

Those who saw the young actress at work very quickly realised that she was a star of the future. Jane Campion and P. J. Hogan, two thrusting young directors spotted Nicole performing at Sydney's Phillip Street Theatre and fought for the right to use her in their graduation films.

Nicole was not at all happy when she was unable to take either role. She had auditioned for a part in Jane Campion's film *A Girl's Own Story*, which was an exploration of female sexuality, and been chosen, but afterwards she was told by her headmistress that she most certainly could not accept it. She was considered too young to take such a break from her studies and the head and her staff were united in their decision that exams were Nicole's first priority. Nicole was deeply disappointed to have to pull out but Campion was understanding and sent her a note: 'I think you made the right decision and I hope one day we will work together. Be careful with what you do, because you have real potential.'

That drama passed but Nicole was in great demand. She landed a starring role in *BMX Bandits*. Producer Tom Broadbridge held auditions all over Australia in search of the young actress to play gutsy biker Judy. He realised Nicole was something special, and even before production had finished on her first major film role, Broadbridge was already predicting stardom in the future.

This popular children's film featured Nicole stunt-cycling her way round the more scenic areas of Manly and freeing the beachfront community from the clutches of some of the clumsiest criminals ever screened while creating new records for the number of scenes including a BMX bike. Nicole played heroine Judy who led two boys fearlessly into action, and effortlessly dominated the film. She was delighted to discover the director, Brian Trenchard-Smith, wanted Judy to be the sort of strong girl that Nicole's mother definitely approved of. 'I really liked acting her,' said Nicole. 'She is very independent and stands up for herself. She is also very brave and very plucky. I liked the scenes where she hits the crooks. Brian wanted Judy to be a strong person, thank goodness. I couldn't have stood playing one of those meek, scared girls you often see in films.' Along with Angelo D'Angelo and James Lugton, the two boys who played Judy's sidekicks PJ and Goose, Nicole was trained to ride BMX bikes for two weeks and was disappointed when stunt riders were brought in to do most of the action scenes.

She did have one scary moment, hiding in an open grave with a rat. But even more alarming was the moment when Goose snatched a stolen kiss with her. Nicole was delighted that the drama did not descend into a soppy romance. 'They all end up as just good friends,' she says. 'They were buddies really. I thought that was much better than Judy being matched up with one of the boys. I wouldn't have liked to see Judy breaking up the boys' really close friendship by becoming either Goose or PJ's girlfriend. Judy is only about fifteen. She is not really ready to be serious about a particular boy. Remember she says, "Two's company, three gets us talked about." I think there she is saying she thinks it is more fun to do things in a group than be with just one boy. Also, I think Judy is a good example to girls because she is the boys' equal and just as involved in all the action as they are. She is also a terrific BMX rider and they really admire her for that.'

The chief villain of the piece was played by popular and

much respected British character actor Bryan Marshall, who now lives in Australia. Bryan recalls the fifteen-year-old Nicole with warmth and admiration. 'Apart from her obvious qualities of looks and personality and talent I was especially impressed by her devotion to the fundamental process of acting and her attachment to theatre work as the basis of it all,' he says. 'She worked with, trained with, and still has strong ties with the Australian Theatre for Young People. *BMX Bandits* was great fun to work on but apart from that, two odd things stand out in my memory. One of the support actors was unlucky enough to come down with hepatitis – which meant that at one point all cast and crew had to line up and lower their daks for an injection! Also, the fight between the forces of good and evil at the end was soft-sold into a flour-bomb fight which went on a bit. Quite a few of us woke up the morning after to find our eyelids glued together with what can only be described as pastry!

'Some time later I attended a dinner and Nicole and her parents were there. I was seated next to Antony Kidman who is an eminent behavioural psychologist and occasional broadcaster. He was interested to know how actors work and prepare for a role so I took him through some of the methods we use and digging we do into the human condition. The degree of this probing into self and others was news to him, and he found it fascinating, especially its close alignment to what he does for a living. An interesting man, a nice bloke and a very proud father.'

The work offers kept coming. Nicole had just turned sixteen when she trekked up to the small Queensland town of Aimkillenbun for a small but important role in the ABC mini-series *Chase Through the Night*. It was a tense story based on Australian writer Max Fatchen's book about a remote country town being taken over by three fleeing bank robbers. John Jarratt was the leading light and he recalls with great affection working with the teenage Nicole. She was very professional and very charming, recalls Jarratt. Nicole played young Petra, who was taken hostage by villains. Nicole did not escape her schoolwork because she was forced to spend a lot of time on the location with her travelling tutor swotting up on her school set text, *Romeo and Juliet*.

In October 1984 a more important break arrived for the ambitious young actress. Nicole landed a part in a series for the Disney Channel called *Five Mile Creek*, which took eight months to film in Melbourne, far away from home. The story was about two women who struggled to establish a way-station in the bush for a coach line. She was seventeen and it meant leaving her home and her school. Although Nicole said: 'Because I am starting as a regular on *Five Mile Creek* I will be doing correspondence and night school and as I am going to be there all year I thought I might as well do my HSC,' she learned a lot more about her chosen career than she did for her HSC and the academic ambitions were swiftly put on hold. Her fondest memories are of learning to love the lens at last. 'It was working on camera six days a week, twelve hours a day,' she says. 'I had always been intimidated by the camera. But it became like second nature. The camera was not this ominous creature and I didn't worry about it ever again.'

Being separated from her family was not a new experience as she had been going away on location since she was fourteen with the full support of her parents. Now her role in *Five Mile Creek* looked as though it might lead to an opportunity to work in the United States.

★ ★ ★

Nicole's acting was making schoolwork more and more difficult
– trying to combine schoolwork with the demands of an actress
was never easy. 'I used to get dragged off the set and piled in
the back of a van by my tutor to do schoolwork,' she said. At
seventeen she decided to leave school and pursue a career in
acting full-time rather than go to college. Although that
decision would have disappointed most parents, Nicole's
mother and father backed her completely though Janelle said :
'Acting is such a wretched business. It is so insecure. It was a
profession Nic forged for herself but I have to say we were
always supportive.' In the difficult early days of her career
Janelle told her daughter to call her on the phone whenever
she felt the need and Nicole drew great strength from her
mother's counselling. But she admitted later that at times she
was a 'nightmare' to her parents. Although there were raised
voices and rows, Nicole still charitably concluded afterwards:
'My parents were always extremely supportive. They allowed
me any artistic outlet I wanted. I was lucky because my parents
were extremely encouraging and I don't think I could have
made the decision to leave school without their support.'
Nicole's family have always been everything to her. She once
said: 'It is my family I am working so hard for. They are just the
most important people in the world.'

Although Nicole remained adamant afterwards that leaving
school was the right decision, she was determined to continue
her education. She took Italian lessons and vowed to go back
one day to university to take up her studies again.

Today Nicole remains deeply grateful that her parents were
so supportive of her dream to become an actress, though it was
never an easy or predictable path she trod. 'My parents thought

it was nice to develop my imagination,' said Nicole. 'But they never seriously thought that anything would come of it.' She was certainly never pushed into acting. 'I was the one doing the pushing,' she says. 'It's great having an academic background at home. There has always been conversation over the dinner table and I have always been encouraged to question. That is great for an actor.' Yet, by the time she was a teenager, she had developed considerable writing skills, and her father encouraged her to think of a career in journalism, so at first she did not think of acting as a full-time career. 'I saw acting as a fantasy career, light, fluffy and not quite possible. I was at North Sydney Girls' High and I was going to be a journalist or a lawyer.' She began keeping a diary which she maintains to this day.

When Nicole was sixteen she travelled all over Europe. She believes she has the voracious appetite for experience possessed by many actors. She knew it was dangerous at times but she would simply steel herself and go for it when it came to doing something exciting or interesting. Men flocked to the teenage traveller and sometimes she responded. Afterwards she knew she had been reckless but she loved the frisson of danger.

Nicole says she has been in love three times in her life and remains friends with all her ex-boyfriends. Boys first entered her consciousness at about fourteen. 'I really started to like them,' she said. 'It's wonderful when that happens. Those tingles are priceless. I spent two years with a man who was thirteen years older than me. I also dated another who was seventeen years older than me. I was seventeen. My parents were quite open.'

At seventeen Nicole went to Amsterdam with a boyfriend.

She said: 'I met a guy, knew him for a month, then got on a plane and went to Amsterdam. It was a huge mistake but I did it and I survived and since then I have always kept on travelling. I love it. I think it is unhealthy to get too settled early on in life so I like to move around.'

In an Amsterdam flea market she found the dress that she would eventually get married in, 'a very simple but very beautiful' antique brocaded gown from the 1930s. She bought the dress many years before she was to wear it. She thought at the time she would marry the man she was with. 'We went to Paris, stayed in a tiny attic room, could barely afford bread and cheese. But boy it was so romantic. We went to Italy, to Florence and it snowed.' Then she laughed in relief that she did not. But they stayed friends though, and she felt sure that he, too, would probably laugh at their lucky escape.

Nicole was in great demand and was snapped up by charismatic writer and director John Duigan to star as a fifteen-year-old 1,500-metre runner in his TV movie *Room to Move*, which was the sixth in a series of eight films for younger viewers called *Winners*, focusing on social issues affecting children first shown in autumn 1986. Nicole played the athlete Carol Trig who was beginning to rebel against her father's strict training regime. Terry Donovan played Carol's stern father and unforgiving coach. Carol encountered a punkish girl called Angie, played by Alyssa Cook, who arrives at her school and the two became friends and spent time eating hamburgers together at the strangely named Armpit café where Carol had to work after school. Angie's father does not care about her enough to spend any time with her and she drops out of school to pursue her dream of becoming a dancer. That leads to Carol discovering dancing and a new way of life away from the track. She manages to come only second in the vital race but does not care because she had made the decision to live her life her way.

Nicole worked well and John Duigan said: 'I was impressed with the way she could apply herself single-mindedly. She has an extraordinary ability to focus on things.' Nicole and Duigan forged a close working relationship based on mutual respect. Nicole said: 'He has this ability to draw things out of people and I suddenly thought, "Oh I love doing this." '

Nicole and Duigan kept in touch throughout her formative early years as an actress and she learned a lot from the award-winning writer–director. She would later forge close bonds with other directors. 'It is inevitable that you get a relationship if you work closely for months. I think it is very important that they get to know you and your moods so they can really direct you.'

The one teenage film that Nicole Kidman will never forget is *Windrider*. She stripped for some explicit love scenes that she prefers not to recall, and the lightweight thriller was dramatically deeply disappointing. But much more important, while making the movie she both met the man who became one of the first great loves of her life and received the most devastating shock of her young life when she was told that her mother had cancer.

Windrider opens with Tom Burlinson as a would-be champion windsurfer known as PC taking his surfboard out on the waves early one morning. Burlinson had burst into the Aussie consciousness in 1982 as *The Man from Snowy River*, and his blond good looks had already helped to turn him into something of an Australian heart-throb. The movie was based on a classic Australian poem by A. B. 'Banjo' Paterson which nearly every

Australian had drummed into him or her as a child. Burlinson's youthful good looks enabled him to convincingly get away with playing an eighteen-year-old, even though he was twenty-five when the film was made. *The Man from Snowy River* was shot in the spectacularly rugged terrain of the Great Dividing Range in Victoria. It is a highly charged rites of passage adventure story and featured Kirk Douglas playing two brothers who have fallen out in a bad way. One, called Harrison, is a wealthy autocratic landowner and the other, Spur, is a gruff, grizzled, out of luck prospector. Tom Burlinson played Jim Craig who proves himself a man during an unforgettable chase on horseback down the rugged Snowy Mountains and becomes a legend. Jim's triumph was largely thanks to his crack horseman and mentor Clancy, who was played by Jack Thompson, one of Australia's most popular actors.

In *Windrider*, Burlinson was the cool and confident PC, a young man determined to windsurf his way to stardom. The movie opens with PC out on the water where, much to his delight, he manages to achieve a classic 360-degree loop on his board. PC returns to the shore to find that the only witness to his feat was a strikingly tall girl with a mass of red ringlets who had been watching from a windswept clifftop. He races up the sand to try to get her name as a witness to his achievement but by the time he gets to the top she has gone.

By day PC works at his father's engineering firm where he spends much of his time trying to design a revolutionary new windsurfing board which will give him the edge in upcoming championships. But one night he spots his clifftop girl once more – and this time he discovers she is an up-and-coming singer in a rock band. She is Jade Kelly, a raunchy rocker dressed in leather skirt, red leather jacket and leather mittens.

He pursues her to a recording studio where she is laying down tracks for an album and audaciously picks her up in a fireman's lift and marches her out of the studio. He soon learns, however, that Jade is ambitious, single-minded and not at all in the mood to be carried away. In no uncertain terms Jade lets PC know that she will not be deflected from wholeheartedly pursuing her dream of rock stardom.

It is clear, though, that she finds the blond, bronzed PC attractive. There is an appealing confidence about him as he drives to the shore every day in his souped-up beach buggy with personalised number plate, PC 360. Eventually, and a shade tediously, Jade and PC get together and fall in love, but then find their divergent interests drive them apart. Much later they are reunited just in time for Jade to see PC become a late but triumphant entry in the world windsurfing championships, beating his deadly rival, Coyote.

The movie called for Nicole to perform her first nude scenes. She looks almost embarrassed in the first in which she is seen taking a shower. Burlinson, stripped to the waist, joins her under the water and kisses her passionately. There is also a scene in which the couple are shown naked on a bed enthusiastically making love. They are most certainly not among Nicole Kidman's favourite screen memories. Four years later, when she was twenty-one, Nicole said politely that she had had a great time making *Windrider* and it was a film that she made, 'Because I wanted to work.'

There are several romantic scenes in which the couple are seen taking a sunset stroll along the shore, cycling together and enjoying a beach barbie. The two actors became close and tried their best to do what they could to improve the film.

During filming Nicole received a telephone call that she can never forget. It was her mother, with shattering news. Nicole told *Rolling Stone* magazine: 'She found a lump in her breast. I remember the day vividly. I was working on *Windrider* and she called me from the hospital where the cancer was diagnosed. I dropped the phone and begged the producers to let me go back and see her. And they said no.'

It was the first major trauma to cloud Nicole's young life and it rocked the whole foundation of her existence. She somehow got through that day. 'Then it was a year in hell,' said Nicole. 'She was very sick. She had a lumpectomy which was new at the time, then chemotherapy and radiation. We thought she was going to die. I moved back into the house. I remember the whole shift very clearly. You encounter something like that and say, "OK, it isn't all going to work out like you want." '

In an interview a few years afterwards, Nicole was asked how close to death she had ever been. She said: 'I've driven on the wrong side of the road, barely nicking the car in front of me. I've been with my mother when she had breast cancer. I was seventeen when she went through chemo. I learned massage therapy to help her through radiation. She is still alive and I am very, very close to her.' It was a terrible shock for the whole family. 'Suddenly the person you love most in the world is losing her hair and sobbing every night,' said Nicole. 'It was very hard to see your mother going through such pain. It opened my eyes to mortality, and to pain and suffering, and from that point on I was determined to support her and in some way help.' The crisis brought out the remarkable strength of character of all the Kidmans.

Typically Nicole still chooses not to go publicly into the hours of support she and the rest of the family gave Janelle or to catalogue her mother's long and brave battle with cancer. If the family was tightly knit before the illness, afterwards the togetherness was almost tangible. A close friend told the authors: 'I have never known a family like the Kidmans. They are four separate people yet they are like parts of the same person. The communication between them is extraordinary. They really care for each other so much. They have always been like that. If you see them together you often see they have the same expression. The family is the most important thing to them, it always has been and it always will be. That is why so long as they always have each other the four Kidmans will always be able to withstand any disaster.'

Janelle's cancer changed the family in profound and lasting ways. Antony Kidman shifted the focus of his work as a result of his wife's illness. He is currently doing a major clinical trial on the effects of cognitive behaviour therapy on women with advanced breast cancer and is working in the burgeoning new field of 'pyschoncology' which helps cancer patients and their families cope better with the disease and its treatment. But happily Janelle did recover and the Kidmans gradually went back to living their lives.

Some time afterwards, after *Windrider* had dimmed in her memory, Nicole slipped over to America for a week to catch up with friends she had made while making the international co-production *Five Mile Creek*. There she met some high-powered showbusiness agents and considered various entreaties to take the plunge. She was very tempted to head straight for Hollywood but decided to wait. Nicole said: 'It is hard trying to decide whether to stay here or head overseas for work. I want to play it by ear at the moment and my agent wants me to stay here for another year. Unfortunately I am the sort of person who wants to do everything at once. I decided I was not really ready for America and the best thing was to come back and concentrate on my work here. Los Angeles is the Mecca if you want to be a big star but Australia is where my family and friends are. I can still work in America but I don't have to live there.'

Nicole Kidman and Tom Burlinson were a glamorous item for more than two years but she always fought hard to maintain her individuality and she retained her own home throughout the relationship. She wanted to be successful in her own right, not for her position on the arm of an older, more experienced actor. For a time success shone on them both and they became Australia's golden couple. Nicole was perfectly relaxed to be sharing her life with a man older than her. 'He was the one who gave me a great belief in men. He was kind and open, he gave me a lot of freedom. And because he was so much older he realised I probably was not going to stay with him. Most men that age would have been insecure and controlling. I was really lucky to have had him.' Her wise and caring parents were not shocked by this relationship. 'My mother would always say, "It's not age, it's people."'

In 1987 Burlinson starred in a sci-fi movie called *The Time Guardian*, playing a fortieth-century soldier. When the film was launched in November 1987, he said: 'We're very happy together and she's an important part of my life.' The long awaited sequel to the movie that made his name arrived the following year. *The Man from Snowy River II* was given a lavish launch in March 1988, with critics flown to the Victoria highlands for a two-day shindig. Nicole was there for Burlinson's big moment. He played a now grown-up Jim Craig. Journalists and guests were treated to a slap-up dinner and a day at the local races as well as the movie premier.

In *Watch the Shadows Dance*, a futuristic telemovie which went out almost completely unnoticed on Channel Nine, Nicole had a strange role. She played one of a weird bunch of students who met up in the middle of the night in Sydney to play bizarre computer games. In spite of portraying ample doses of drug-taking and violence it disappeared largely without trace. Nicole's remarkable gift for salvaging some personal credit from a screen failure served her well, as the Sydney *Morning Herald* noted that she was 'pretty terrific in an awful drama'. The role that would turn her from a promising youngster into an Australian icon was just around the corner.

Vietnam was a huge project from the high-quality Kennedy–Miller production stable. John Duigan enthused to writer Terry Hayes about the remarkable teenage talent of Nicole Kidman who had appeared in his *Winners* film. Hayes was plotting *Vietnam*, a powerful new television drama serial that would explore Australia's controversial involvement in the Vietnam War of the early 1970s. The character of Megan Goddard, who developed through the epic story from an awkward fourteen-year-old schoolgirl into an outspoken and free-thinking 24-year-old protester, was absolutely crucial to the success of the project.

There were some extraordinary parallels with Nicole's own life. In one scene Megan cries: 'Five feet nine! Nobody's going to ask me out to the dance.' 'But men like tall women,' says Mrs Goddard, trying to boost her daughter's fragile, teenage ego. 'Yeah, men do, but I want boys. And boys like short girls with big norks,' Megan replies with appropriate hand gestures. 'If only I was voluptuous.' Not surprisingly Nicole Kidman played the scene perfectly, thanks no doubt to the fact that she had plenty of real life practice.

Vietnam changed Nicole's life for ever. It was her first real major performance fleshing out comic and dramatic roles as she took the character of Megan Goddard on her compelling journey. It was not a surprise to the actress. 'I knew that *Vietnam* was going to be great,' says Nicole. 'I knew because I had worked with John Duigan the director before and because it was a Kennedy–Miller production. I remember when they rang and said I'd got the part I screamed. I was so excited. I knew that I had finally got a role that was three-dimensional.'

Nicole, then nineteen, was not even born when the Beatles first became popular so she had to research the life and culture of the 1960s. Her character, Megan, lived through the years from 1964 to 1972 and Nicole said: 'My parents couldn't help me much because they lived in America then. We had seminars and lectures from Jim Cairns and Simon Townsend, so we could learn about the controversy of sending Australian troops to Vietnam.'

Cairns had led moratorium marches against conscription while Townsend was a high-profile draft dodger who did time for burning his draft card. Nicole was surprised to learn that sixties teenagers were more politically aware than those of the eighties. 'It was a great period of change,' she said. 'I slowly caught up with the sixties. Of course the *Vietnam* directors, Chris Noonan and John Duigan, helped me. And Terry Hayes, the scriptwriter and producer, was bubbling with encouragement. After doing all that reading and filming the series, I came out firmly on the side of Megan. I couldn't see the sense in sending Australians out there. Megan goes through a real awakening. She starts out being interested in sex and drugs and gradually realises that there is much more to life than fun. It was a great period of change. I think people are more insular now. They have forgotten that people can change the world.' Nicole was sad that teenagers seemed so much more conservative then than their predecessors of two decades earlier. She said: 'They think if they pay their twenty dollars to go to a Live Aid concert they have done their bit. Dad brought me up to have a liberal, open-minded outlook. I am politically aware now, I have been since the late seventies. I make it part of my job to read the papers and discuss things. Otherwise you are ignorant.'

The dramatic high point of *Vietnam* comes when Megan is a guest on a radio phone-in show protesting against the horrors of conscription. When a recently returned Vietnam veteran calls the programme to question her arguments, Megan recognises her estranged brother's voice and breaks down in sobs. It is a poignant moment that was extremely difficult to achieve. Nicole did that scene in a single take. A six-minute segment, one long facial reaction, not having seen her brother in a long time and finally recognising his voice. To this day it is the scene many people remember when they think of her. 'Watching her,' says John Duigan, 'there wasn't a dry eye in the whole country.' Terry Hayes was spellbound. He said: 'That was real acting. I mean some actresses might be able to find that once. Or they could go in and out of it. But Nicole could do it time after time after time and it was better each time. When we were sitting there later that night watching the rushes the whole crew just applauded. And that is very rare.' Nicole refused to be carried away by all the enthusiasm. She loved the series certainly, but when pushed later, she rated her performance as worth only five or six out of ten. 'But I am very critical of myself,' said Nicole. 'I know when I have done something wrong. I know myself back to front and inside out.'

Producer–director George Miller knew that Nicole Kidman was destined to be an international star as soon as he saw the rushes for *Vietnam*. 'I take a certain amount of credit for her success because the thing that turned her into a serious actress was her role in *Vietnam*,' says George. 'Until then she had made only a few children's movies. I still remember her scene in *Vietnam* where she made that extraordinary anti-war speech to her brother. It was very powerful. I immediately saw her potential. For me it was the same when I first saw Mel Gibson's screen test for *Mad Max* and Michelle Pfeiffer's for *Witches of Eastwick*. Every now and then in your life you come across a very special talent. When it happens you are inclined to remember.'

Nicole had got the job because John Duigan had convinced Terry Hayes that she really was something special. Later, after the worldwide success of *Vietnam* had more than justified Duigan's faith in Kidman, Hayes said: 'It is extraordinarily rare that not only do you have beauty and talent but that it is so highly developed in a person of her age. I keep forgetting that she is only twenty-one. That makes her in a group of one at the moment, not just in Australia but in the world. That is the kind of advantage she had and boy is she going to make it, you just watch her.'

Nicole won an Australian Film Institute award for best actress in a mini-series for her performance as Megan, as well as the Logie for most popular actress in a mini-series. She was not in Australia to collect her awards. Instead she was enjoying a few weeks in Britain with boyfriend Tom Burlinson before she returned to begin rehearsals on her first major stage play, a production of *Steel Magnolias* that was due to open in Sydney on 1 May 1988. 'I was travelling in Scotland. It was better not to be there,' she said. 'Terry Hayes gave a wonderful speech and left a bit of mystery in the air and that was it. I think it is better than me getting up and saying "Oh thank you, thank you". I would do it certainly, if I had the chance, but rather than sitting around seeing if you have won awards I think it is much better to be working or travelling or getting on with your life.'

After *Vietnam*, Nicole considered going to the acclaimed Australian National Institute of Dramatic Art in the footsteps of Mel Gibson and Judy Davis. But John Duigan advised her against it. She recalls: 'He said, "Don't go, they will destroy you," so I never went. I always think I would have loved to have gone because I love being around actors. I love talking about acting and I wanted to go to college but he said, "Don't go." So I chose the other route which was to work, work, work.'

Vietnam was a fabulous project for Nicole Kidman, and from then on there was never the slightest doubt about the path she was going to follow. Win or lose she was going to stick with acting.

'During the making of *Vietnam* I had my own pad and was really on my own for the first time, doing cooking and housekeeping. It was my dream to have my own place and be my own person. My parents had mixed feelings and there was definite tension about my not going to college – with my father especially. But I was not going to be sidetracked. That mini-series opened so many doors. Without it I would probably have drifted along and maybe done a couple of unmemorable film parts until I lost heart and then just faded away. But then I was offered *Dead Calm.'*

CHAPTER 4

Between the Devil and the Deep Blue Sea

*'Within days it was like sharks at a feeding frenzy with
agents trying to sign her'*
– DEAD CALM PRODUCER GEORGE MILLER AFTER
THE MOVIE'S FIRST SCREENING IN AMERICA

I n 1963, four years before Nicole Kidman was born, a novel
entitled *Dead Calm* by Charles Williams hit the bookstalls. It
was the chilling tale of a terrifying tug-of-war played out at
sea between a happily married couple enjoying a leisurely
cruise and a madman who seizes control of their yacht.

More than twenty years later, a film based on the book
was destined to change nineteen-year-old Nicole Kidman's
life for ever. It would prove not just a springboard to
international movie stardom but would indirectly project her
into the arms of one of Hollywood's top male movie icons –
Tom Cruise.

First to spot *Dead Calm*'s potential as a movie was Desi Arnaz, a diminutive but explosive Cuban who had begun his career as a singer, performed in minor musicals, and then married comedienne Lucille Ball, before going on to become a powerful player in Hollywood. Arnaz was quick to snap up the rights soon after *Dead Calm* was published, but before long they had transferred to Orson Welles, the ebullient American actor–writer–producer–director. Welles had panicked the whole of America in 1938 with a vivid radio version of *The War of the Worlds* and he saw *Dead Calm* as a means of repeating a similarly chilling experience for cinema audiences.

By the time Welles was enthusing about his project, the aura that had surrounded him since his classic movie *Citizen Kane* had dimmed in the eyes of the Hollywood power brokers. His extravagance and unconventionality had long since forced him to Europe where his projects continued to be interesting and ambitious. So it was to the Dalmatian coast of Yugoslavia that he set out in 1968 with his long-standing companion Oja Kodar, a sculptress and actress, to film *Dead Calm* under the title of *The Deep*. In the principal roles were Oja and Michael Bryant as Rae and John Ingram, the cruising couple whose idyll is so terrifyingly shattered, and Laurence Harvey as the unhinged aggressor Hughie Warriner. Also in the cast was formidable French actress Jeanne Moreau.

By this stage of his career, Welles had gained a reputation for being generally undisciplined and for leaving behind a series of projects, such as *Don Quixote*, which remained half finished or unreleased. *The Deep* was destined to become one such movie. Filming began in 1969, but the death of Laurence Harvey eventually caused Welles to abandon his project, claiming it unfinished although, according to Jeanne Moreau, Welles had in fact completed it. Some said that Welles actually suppressed it but, whatever the truth of the matter, *The Deep* remained in the Orson Welles vaults.

As time went by, its non-appearance served only to spur other film-makers' interest in *Dead Calm*. Many producers remained fascinated by the story and its cinematic potential, but efforts to bring it to the screen after Welles's death were thwarted by Oja Kodar, who was reluctant to sell the rights to Hollywood after Tinseltown's treatment of Orson. She blamed Hollywood for many of Orson's troubles.

Eventually Tony Bill, producer of the hugely successful Robert Redford–Paul Newman movie *The Sting*, took an interest. Then, generously as it eventually turned out, in 1984 Bill gave a copy of *Dead Calm* to Australian director Phillip Noyce, explaining that he felt it was a movie project ideally suited to Australia because of its vast surrounding expanses of sea.

Noyce remembers putting the book in his briefcase and carrying it around for six months before seriously examining its screen possibilities. He was busy working in the US on a drama series called *The Hitchhiker*, a series of one-off morality tales similar to *Alfred Hitchcock Presents*, when he came to realise the book's potential.

Once he had become excited about its possibilities, Noyce began pursuing the rights in earnest and discovered they were part of the estate left by Orson Welles that included five unfinished or unreleased films. But he was gratified to find that Oja Kodar welcomed his interest in *Dead Calm* with open arms. She was delighted that someone other than a Hollywood studio would remake the movie. Noyce had started out making left-leaning films and Oja regarded the Kennedy–Miller organisation as being the kind of maverick outfit of which Orson Welles himself would have heartily approved.

Noyce had been born in a small town in New South Wales where his father not only farmed but also practised law. He had first become interested in movies in his teens after watching a series of experimental so-called 'underground movies' and realising that films did not have to be British or made in Hollywood – the general fare then served up at Australian cinemas.

He made his first film in his final year at school, cleverly bankrolling it by charging his friends to appear in it with the promise that the bigger the investment, the bigger the role would be. He went on to study Law at Sydney University then switched to major in Fine Arts. In his spare time he made use of the Sydney University Film Society's equipment, which gave him the impetus to go on to study film direction at the Australian National Film School in its inaugural year in 1973.

From there, Noyce went on to make his name by directing *Newsfront*, one of Australia's most popular movies, which celebrated newsreel cameramen; *Heatwave*, starring Judy Davis, which took a swipe at urban developers; *The Cowra Breakout*, a critique of Aussie treatment of Japanese prisoners of war; and *The Dismissal*, a drama about the fall of Australia's first Socialist government.

When it came to considerations of casting *Dead Calm*, the name of Nicole Kidman was the last one to spring to Noyce's mind. In the novel, Rae was a 36-year-old woman and Noyce naturally envisioned an established movie actress around that age in the lead role, a formidable star, perhaps, of the status of Meryl Streep or Sigourney Weaver. Logically, Nicole was totally unsuitable as she was then only nineteen years old, just over half the age of the central character.

Also weighing heavily against Nicole was a far more important disadvantage than her tender years. Quite simply,

Noyce had barely heard of Nicole Kidman. Her name meant virtually nothing to him because he had been in America working on various projects when Nicole had first made such an impact on TV in Australia in the mini-series *Vietnam*.

With a substantial $10 million budget in place and the backing of Warner Bros as distributors in America, Noyce and producer George Miller could afford to woo a Hollywood name for the female lead. But Terry Hayes, who was writing *Dead Calm* for the screen, had other ideas. As he worked on the screenplay, he kept thinking about Nicole for the role of Rae. Eventually he argued with Miller and Noyce that they could chase Meryl Streep, Debra Winger or Sigourney Weaver, or indeed any other top Hollywood actress, but when it came down to talent they should at least consider Nicole. To back up his argument he urged Noyce at least to take a look at her performance in *Vietnam*, particularly the scene where her character, the feisty Megan Goddard, breaks down in tears while talking to her brother on a radio phone-in show.

The tall, well-built and bearded Noyce was suitably impressed and was almost moved to tears himself by the radio scene. He readily agreed to test Nicole. 'Once we'd screen-tested her, it was hard to see anyone else in the part,' he said. 'We had our choice of any actress really, even someone with a big box-office name. But I looked at tapes of Nicole in the mini-series *Vietnam* and felt she had the purity we were looking for. She had to show a certain guile and yet needed to be a woman that women can love. Nicole had beauty and sexuality and innocence and vulnerability. Once I saw *Vietnam* I believed in Nicole so firmly, I was totally prepared to suffer the consequences of not having a "name" actress in that role.'

Nicole was initially consumed with self-doubt about her suitability for the part. She worried that she was not up to the task of playing Rae. She could see it was an immensely demanding role, not least physically, for an actress of her limited experience. She also worried about whether Sam Neill, a handsome, established, competent actor, who had signed to play her husband John Ingram, would get on with her. Neill was joining *Dead Calm* on the back of starring with Meryl Streep in *Evil Angels* and Nicole was more than a little in awe of the New Zealander who, aged forty, was over twice her age and something of a heart-throb.

Emboldened by the faith that Miller, Noyce and Hayes were prepared to place in her, she decided it was a challenge far too good to turn down once she was assured that the age difference between Rae and John would be turned into a positive element of the couple's relationship. Any exploration of the age difference was considered unnecessary and two lines of dialogue in which Sam Neill's character John explains: 'She's not my daughter, she's my wife' were reportedly removed.

Rae Ingram was obviously a terrific part for a woman – unusually so for Australian movies. As Nicole was not slow to grasp, a lot of Australian films had focused on Australia's history and were therefore male-oriented. But here was a role of a woman struggling to overcome incredible odds and Nicole knew that every actress in Australia would want it.

There was also the broader picture to consider. *Dead Calm* had sizeable financial backing and solid Hollywood involvement and would be made by a committed team with a decent track record. It was clearly destined to have a wider impact on her career than her work hitherto. Rae Ingram, she concluded, was a role she simply could not refuse. 'It had prestige around it and it had a good budget; it was going to be a big film and it had a Warner Bros release in the US,' she said.

For the role of the crazed murderer Hughie Warriner, the choice came down to Chicago-born Billy Zane, at twenty-one an up-and-coming actor whose dark good looks were winning him comparisons with a young Marlon Brando. Ironically, it was to be another seagoing movie, *Titanic*, some twelve years later, in which he played the villain to Kate Winslet's Rose, which would make him a true international star.

Zane came to *Dead Calm* after small but noticeable roles in the movies *Back to the Future*, and *Critters*. Six feet two inches tall and powerfully built, he was necessarily quite a bit taller than Nicole to ensure he looked capable of physically overpowering her in any battle of strength.

Any qualms Nicole may have had about working with Sam Neill were quickly eased when she had dinner with the man who was to play her screen husband. They both came away from the meal knowing they would get on well together. 'She's a very clever and talented girl, very sexy and she's fun,' was Neill's eventual verdict on his co-star.

Buoyed by this confidence, Nicole threw herself whole-heartedly into an intensive course of preparation to play Rae. Determined to look and behave as realistically as possible as Neill's wife, Nicole made a study of posture so she could carry herself like an older woman and even went through voice training so that her voice sounded older. She also added some weight to her slender, girlish figure.

Eager to get inside the mind of Rae, Nicole sought out naval wives to talk to and even mothers who had suffered the trauma of losing a child. She concentrated hard on trying to imagine what it must be like for a mother to suffer such a terrible loss and immersed herself so deeply in reaching for that emotion that one week before filming started she awoke from a dream and in her drowsy state really did believe for a second or two that she had a little boy of her own lying in bed beside her.

On a practical level, she spent one month with a sailing instructor who taught her how to bring a 20-metre yacht into the wind and across it. 'On the first day of training I crashed the yacht into one of the tender boats that was following along,' Nicole remembers. 'You should have heard the abuse I got from the Italian captain.'

Nicole worked closely with Terry Hayes and Phillip Noyce on building Rae's character through its various stages – the devastation of a mother losing her child, the terror of finding herself at the mercy of a deranged killer and the determination to survive and save her husband. 'It was very much developed so that I wasn't to be just the damsel in distress,' Nicole noted. 'Rae grows and finds inner strength through her ordeal. The role required me to find emotions that were not necessarily emotions I had experienced. Life, fear, frustration, terror, the loss of a child. At the beginning she is fragile and weak, but the ordeal changes her. She finds an inner strength.'

Noyce saw it as 'a rite of passage', with Rae going from weakness to power, from girlhood to womanhood, from loss to re-growth. Although suspense was to be a key component of *Dead Calm*, Noyce saw the underlying element of the movie as a love story. He had been particularly moved in the book by the desire of the husband and wife to be reunited and was anxious that anything that removed the focus from that would dissipate the drama and the emotional involvement with the story. 'The love the husband and wife have for each other sustains all the other elements,' he stressed. 'The suspense comes into it – will they survive to get back together again? – and the thrills are along the way. But at heart it still remains a love story.'

It was within these parameters that Hayes set out to write the chilling story which would open on a tragic note with a car crash in which a young boy is killed as his mother, Rae Ingram, drives him to meet her naval officer husband John at Central Station. She herself is badly injured and, when she eventually recovers, the couple take off on what they hope will be a recuperative holiday cruise together in isolated waters on their luxury yacht *Saracen* in a bid to forget the trauma.

Suddenly one fine day their solitude is broken. There is something on the horizon. Their pet dog alerts them to a man in a dinghy rowing frantically away from a schooner and towards their yacht. They help him on board and he collapses from exhaustion. Barely coherent, he blurts out a story that his name is Hughie Warriner and that his companions on the schooner have all died from food poisoning. He is the sole survivor, he says, and his vessel is sinking. He warns the couple not to try to board the stylish sailing vessel which sits ominously several hundred yards away.

John is sceptical, his suspicions are aroused and, while Hughie sleeps, he takes off to explore Hughie's yacht *Orpheus*. There he makes the most grisly discovery of several dead bodies and a videotape which makes it plain that Hughie is responsible for the violent deaths of all the charter passengers on his boat.

Meanwhile, back on *Saracen*, Hughie has soon recovered and reveals himself to Rae to be a complete psychotic, a lunatic with the meanest of streaks. Chillingly, he takes over control of the *Saracen* from a terrified Rae and sails away, leaving John stranded on the slowly sinking *Orpheus* and fearfully watching

Hughie at the helm of his boat, while his wife is lying unconscious hanging over the side.

Trapped between the devil and the deep blue sea, Rae at first tries to distract, then subdue the increasingly dangerous Hughie, while secretly contacting John on the *Orpheus* radio. When she is at the end of her tether and her life is threatened, she feigns an attraction for Hughie and initiates sex with him in order to survive. Despite several opportunities to kill Hughie with shotgun and harpoon gun, she cannot bring herself to do it, preferring instead to lock him in a cabin and then direct all her energies into turning *Saracen* around to meet up once again with John. This she achieves in the nick of time and together they face a terrifying conclusion as Hughie breaks free before finally meeting his fate.

As Nicole read Terry Hayes's script, she was under no illusion that the five-month shoot ahead of her was going to be anything less than physically and emotionally draining. On the face of it, *Dead Calm* appeared to be a simple film to make, featuring as it did just three main characters, one dog and two boats. But in reality it was anything but – right from the first test shots in Sydney harbour where the water was so rough that actors and crew became horribly seasick and ended up vomiting over the side of the boat. Sam Neill, especially, was to find himself prone to queasiness at sea. Many was the time in the weeks ahead filming on a rolling sea that he would turn a sickly shade of green.

Eventually the production headed for the Whitsunday Passage off the north-eastern coast of Queensland where they spent weeks at a time living on a flotilla. Filming started on 19 May 1987, and mainly took place inside a large reef which broke the huge open swells and bordered nearby Hamilton

Island, where cast and crew gratefully headed periodically for sanctuary and the comforts of terra firma when schedules permitted.

There, Nicole discovered a club where she could enjoy a drink, unwind and loosen up on a Saturday night by dancing the twist, the madison and the locomotion to the tunes of the sixties favoured by the club's DJ. In time she became bold enough to drag Sam Neill on to the dance floor to partner her in the sixties dance moves she had learned when researching her role in *Vietnam*.

Noyce encouraged and fostered a situation whereby Nicole and Sam Neill could enjoy a warm friendship off screen while Billy Zane remained distant from Nicole. It all helped to inject the required emotions on screen. Zane considered Nicole beautiful and sexy when he was first introduced to her. But there was never any danger that they would become an item on set once Zane had set eyes very early on in the production on striking blonde Australian model and actress Lisa Collins. Quite literally it was love at first sight.

Lisa had a small role in *Dead Calm* playing one of the wildly uninhibited good-time cruise girls on Hughie Warriner's doomed schooner *Orpheus* who winds up murdered, a dismembered victim of Hughie's crazed brutality. From the moment Zane and Lisa set eyes on each other on set, there was a noticeable sexual electricity crackling between them. It was not long before they became lovers, and within three weeks they announced to an astonished cast and crew that they were engaged to be married. Zane, who had arrived on the set with his head full of a character hell-bent on messing up another woman's life, was grateful for the counter-balance of enjoying a dizzy, passionate, whirlwind real life love affair with a woman he so swiftly knew he wanted to make his wife. Zane and Lisa went on to wed in Hollywood six months later.

A less gifted or committed director than Phillip Noyce might have been overwhelmed by the elements and the sheer unpredictability of the weather when shooting *Dead Calm*. Abrupt changes in ocean weather would play havoc with the shooting schedule, darkening the water and sky in a flash. It could be cloudless and calm as a millpond one minute, choppy underneath an angry, black sky the next. As a counter-measure, Noyce fed his shooting script into a computer system which allowed him to match up his shots to the brooding scenery, the shifting light and varying seas. By cross-indexing his shots, quick switches could be made and appropriate scenes swiftly found when he encountered sudden doldrums or squalls.

For Nicole, apart from the seasickness and filming in a close environment for six to nine hours a day six, sometimes seven, days a week, there was the painful problem of fighting the effects of the scorching sun on her pale skin. 'I spent a tremendous amount of time trying to keep from getting burned,' she said. One day it was pouring with rain and Nicole had been out sailing for five hours. On the way back a storm blew up and she spent ten thoroughly wretched minutes throwing up over the side. 'I couldn't work,' she says. 'I thought: yeah, that's glamour!'

Knowing she worked best when she was well rested, Nicole generally retired to bed early at the end of each day, aiming for ten hours sleep a night. 'We filmed from sun up to sun down. The weather was hot and sticky. We were all drained and exhausted.'

One bright and welcome interlude for Nicole came with the marking of her twentieth birthday. The production team laid on a party for her, and Nicole's boyfriend Tom Burlinson came up to Hamilton Island to join her for a celebration with a few friends.

Apart from climbing up the mast, which was deemed too risky, Nicole threw herself into doing all her own stunts. Neither she nor Zane took the soft option when it came to their cat-and-mouse chases and physical confrontations on the yacht. They grappled and scrapped with unyielding gusto and Nicole emerged with numerous bruises to show for it. At least they counted towards the realism, she could console herself. 'I've never been so bruised in my life,' said Nicole. 'But I was quite proud to pull my jeans off when I was wearing shorts and shock people with my bruises.'

Emotionally, *Dead Calm* was just as demanding for Nicole. The movie's most controversial scene occurs when Rae, having realised just how crazily violent Hughie is, offers herself to him sexually. It is virtually rape, although Hughie deludes himself into believing Rae is eager and willing. She has simply come to the conclusion that having sex with him is probably her best chance of staying alive and of surviving long enough to buy time for her husband to attempt a rescue.

'This is an extremely difficult role for any actress,' George Miller conceded. 'It requires great sensitivity because of the emotions Nicole is required to show. She loves her husband but she must also be able to convince Hughie that she is willing to love him. And at the same time, when she is having sex with Billy, she must let the audience know she is only doing it in an effort to beat him so she can get back to her husband.'

Nicole had no objection to the nudity and simulated sex scene, confident that the focus was on her face, not on her body. The rape is seen through the reactions on her face. 'It's better than being in a film where all your brains fall out all over the place,' she explained. 'I was aware from the script it was going to be a nude sex scene. In the end I didn't find it difficult. I felt in a safe environment. What was difficult was my face had to show the hate and revulsion I felt for that man although I was in a passionate embrace with him. It was a brave act, because what Rae was doing might mean the survival of her husband. You have this very vulnerable almost broken woman who is suddenly put into a situation that could smash her apart emotionally once and for all. But if she lets that happen she knows her husband will die as well so she has to hold herself together and defeat this lunatic even if it means feigning love for him. It's only by holding herself together through this extreme experience that she is able to overcome her tragedy and grow to a position where she can go on with her life.'

Miller additionally pointed out that another important aspect of Nicole's role was to make Rae a woman unwilling to commit violence, unwilling to kill Hughie. 'If this were an American film, they would just hand the heroine a shotgun and let her blow Hughie away,' he explained. 'There was a feeling with *Dead Calm* that we wanted to make this more real. It's not an easy thing for a person to go out and deliberately kill someone unless they are crazy. So it was decided that Nicole would do everything possible to beat Billy without killing him.'

Phillip Noyce's *Dead Calm* emerged as a stylish and intense thriller with echoes of master of suspense Alfred Hitchcock's 1946 movie *Notorious* and Roman Polanski's *Knife in the Water*. Noyce was gracious enough to admit that *Notorious* had been a big influence. In *Notorious*, Ingrid Bergman had to make sexual compromises to try to trap master spy Claude Rains — she married him — while the US agent who loves her, played by

Cary Grant, has to look on helplessly. Noyce said he had been impressed by the way Hitchcock was able to generate in *Notorious* a great deal of suspense without resorting to fast editing, flashy lighting, dramatic music or the gruesome shocks so prevalent in thrillers and horror films of the time. 'It was a case of less is more,' said Noyce.

When Warner Bros screen-tested the movie across the US, they found audiences took Nicole to their hearts, and became utterly caught up in the drama, many screaming at the screen for Nicole not to trust Hughie. Disturbingly for Noyce, who took an active interest in the way the film would be marketed in America, some of the audiences were prone to shouting vociferously for Hughie's blood as Rae became increasingly desperate. At a late-night screening at Grauman's Chinese Theater on Hollywood Boulevard there were chants of 'Kill . . . Kill . . . Kill' when Nicole seized the harpoon gun and was poised to let fly. Noyce attributed their bloodthirsty enthusiasm to the American psyche, that what Americans possessed they were prepared to protect – with violence if necessary – especially when their own safety was threatened. In *Dead Calm*, Hughie was regarded by Americans as an intruder who had violated the Ingrams and should be blown away.

What became increasingly clear from the test screenings was that *Dead Calm* was likely to be a huge success and that it would sweep Nicole Kidman to global stardom. 'The camera loves her. She's going to be a big international star. There's no doubt about it,' Noyce predicted. 'Working with Nicole is a joy. I don't know whether it's just because she's young and hasn't yet learned how to mistrust. But she always listens and tackles everything you tell her with incredible enthusiasm. Only God knows how a teenager could so convincingly play all the complex emotions experienced by the character of Rae, a mature woman, during the course of the story.' He added prophetically: 'It's this ability to be a man's woman and a woman's woman which makes Nicole so extraordinary. I shudder to think what she will be like in ten years if she continues to develop like this.'

Terry Hayes believed Nicole had a rare quality that he had, similarly, found in Mel Gibson. Mel, he said, never had much interest in being a screen star, he was only ever interested in being a great actor. It was the same with Nicole, he noted. Rather than wanting to be a screen goddess, Nicole, he felt, had a fierce commitment to the craft of acting and to the roles she was playing.

George Miller can recall the extraordinarily enthusiastic reaction to Nicole the first time *Dead Calm* was shown to executives at Warner Brothers.

Miller, Noyce and Hayes were all relieved when Sam Cohn, who had flown to Los Angeles specifically to have a breakfast meeting with Nicole, was chosen to represent her. They felt that Cohn, a revered agent who handled the careers of Meryl Streep, Woody Allen and Sigourney Weaver among others, was the kind of agent who would be there for her for the long term rather than seeking to cash in quickly on what was sure to be Nicole's success in *Dead Calm*.

Nicole's inevitable rise to international stardom was something Terry Hayes had predicted and foreseen long before. As one of her great mentors, he naturally felt protective of her and did not want to see her prodigious talent muddied by the big-money offers now coming her way, nor by having her head turned by being signed up by a superagent one day and being taken to lunch by Warren Beatty the next, nor by being constantly told that she was an exceptionally beautiful woman with glossy magazines regularly confirming that view by putting her face on their covers. 'She is, most unusually, an extremely nice person,' Hayes emphasised to one interviewer.

During the filming of *Dead Calm* Hayes told the actress: 'Nicole, whatever happens with this film, it will do two things: it will launch the acting career of Nicole Kidman and it will put Phil Noyce into the front league of film directors in the world.'

Hayes was so utterly convinced that *Dead Calm* would secure a great future for Nicole as a movie actress that he there and then expressed a desire to collaborate with her on one more project before fame took her to a totally different, possibly no longer reachable, level in Hollywood. He vowed to create a mini-series for her if she would commit to what he described as a female version of *Midnight Express*, the powerful 1978 movie about a young American arrested in Turkey for smuggling hashish and his subsequent harsh imprisonment and later escape. It would, he promised, provide Nicole with a role that would stretch her acting abilities to the limit.

According to Hayes, Nicole agreed on just one condition: 'I'll do it,' she said, 'but just promise me one thing. You won't wimp out. You won't leave out all the tough scenes. I want you to really push me as an actress.' Hayes was adamant. 'That's a deal,' he said and set about writing a series called *Bangkok Hilton* for his young protégée.

Warner Bros were so confident that *Dead Calm* would be a box-office and critical success that they decided the film should open in the US before being released in cinemas in Australia. Their faith was rewarded when the film took $3 million at the box office in its first weekend and became the sixth-highest grossing film in the US. Reviews were excellent with Nicole consistently praised for her performance. Hollywood, a town of types, had to agree that she was an original. But anxious as ever to pigeonhole newcomers, the description of Nicole as 'the Australian Sigourney Weaver' was soon being bandied about, partly because of Nicole's height and curls. British critics were also fulsome in their praise for both the film and Nicole when *Dead Calm* opened in London.

Reviewers called *Dead Calm* a stylish thriller that swept the audience along on a gripping wave of terror, danger and adventure without let up. They commented on Noyce's ability to double the suspense by worrying not just about what the audience are seeing on screen but about what they do not see. While Rae was desperately fighting for her life, viewers were also fearing for her unseen husband John, facing a watery grave trapped up to his neck in the bowels of Hughie's doomed yacht. When the action switched to John, the audience could not help but wonder what manner of tortures Rae was being subjected to.

By the time *Dead Calm* reached Australia in May 1989, almost exactly two years to the day since she had started work on it, the movie had proved an unqualified success in America and Nicole was being hailed as 'the next big thing'.

Just prior to the Australian premiere, Nicole spent some time in the States experiencing for the first time the star treatment accorded to major movie idols. In her early days in Los Angeles courtesy of Warner Brothers, she was able to base herself at the luxurious St James Club and a limousine was put at her disposal around the clock. Nothing, she was assured, would be too much trouble. All she had to do was ask. She found the experience hard to cope with and felt she could understand people going off the rails. 'One minute you are travelling around the world first class, staying in the best hotels as though you are a multi-millionaire,' she said. 'The next minute you come back and you have got your old bomb of a car and you are not working and you can't afford to go out for dinner. So you have got these incredible extremes in your life which make it really hard to cope with. You can't get too attached to the luxury of it all. If you do get to like it too much it can be dangerous. When I was over in the States Warner Brothers treated me like you would never believe. I had limousines all the time at my disposal. They had two suites for me and they asked me which one I preferred. I said I don't care, whatever you think. It is so strange. They are continually saying "Is there anything you want? Is there anything you want? You're looking a little stressed would you like a massage, why don't we get a masseuse up here?" And it is very hard to cope with all the attention without feeling so guilty. You end up walking round feeling, "My God, I just don't deserve all this." '

The hard work came when Nicole went on a promotional tour for *Dead Calm*, subjecting herself to up to twenty-five press interviews a day. Almost every interviewer reminded her that she was a rarity – an Australian actress who was setting the screen alight. Until Nicole, it was repeatedly pointed out to her, all the other Australians to have made it to Hollywood had been men: Mel Gibson, Paul Hogan, and going back many years, Peter Finch and Errol Flynn.

Australians, famous for the 'tall poppy syndrome' – they like to cut down to size anyone whom they deem to be rising above themselves – might have been waiting for Nicole to take a fall after the Kidman hype in America. But they, too, flocked to see *Dead Calm* and seemed genuinely pleased for her that she had triumphed in such a difficult role.

All the fuss over their daughter proved somewhat baffling for Antony and Janelle Kidman. Nicole cited an odd moment when her father was lecturing in Brisbane and a member of his audience raised his hand to ask not some meaningful, philosophically challenging question but 'Are you the father of Nicole Kidman?' Nicole cringed at the thought that after her father had spent ten years at university and obtained a PhD all someone wanted to know from him in the middle of one of his lectures was whether she was his daughter.

So-called stardom, she pondered, made for some strange situations. One thing she was becoming acutely aware of was that life after *Dead Calm* was never going to be the same again. 'I was in Grace Brothers store buying lingerie,' she announced, 'and I got these guys coming up to me and asking for my autograph. So I put down the bra and pants and said, "Sure." ' Fan worship was something she was going to have to get used to.

Over in Los Angeles, unbeknown to Nicole, one of the world's greatest movie idols had also become a fan. Tom Cruise, watching *Dead Calm* at a private viewing theatre with his actor friend Emilio Estevez, liked what he was seeing on the screen. 'Who is that girl?' Hollywood's *Top Gun* star enquired of his friend. 'I don't know,' came the reply.

Before so very long Tom Cruise was to know that girl as his wife.

✶

CHAPTER 5

The Bangkok Hilton

*'Life is short. You do not have much time so you must
follow your own star. That may sound selfish but it is not
meant to be. It is just what my mother always said to me:
"Whatever you do in life, don't give up on your dreams"'*
– NICOLE KIDMAN

Nicole was happy to be back home after filming a TV
movie called *An Australian in Rome*. It had been a
difficult job: 'It was hard. It was so hard because I was
working with an all-Italian crew and an Italian director who did
not speak English. They have a completely different style of
work. They dub everything and much to my dismay they
might use another voice to dub my part.'

The film starred Nicole as an innocent youngster. 'Imagine, I
was paid to sightsee all over Italy for two weeks before
shooting even started.' Her character is an Australian girl, in
Rome for the first time. 'Jill is twenty-two and quite naïve but
by the end of the movie she has learned about love and become

rather cynical,' said Nicole enthusiastically. 'It's about a love triangle which develops between Jill and two brothers. I had to scream and cry a lot and endure a lot of mental torture. The movie is very Italian, by that I mean passionate. My two co-stars are delicious and I am learning a lot about Italian men. They definitely don't like skinny women and have been trying to make me put on weight since I arrived here.'

After the fourteen-week shoot of *Dead Calm* Nicole spent time with her boyfriend Tom Burlinson and started work renovating her newly acquired Mosman flat. 'I have just been determined to get a place of my own by the time I was twenty and I was twenty on 20 June so I scraped in.' It did not herald a split from her family. Nicole's mother Janelle helped to find the flat and organised the refurbishing, supervising the laying of the pink and grey carpet and the installation of the art deco lights. Janelle said: 'Actually I would really like to revamp the flat from scratch. I found it for Nicki and so I have a sort of proprietorial interest in it.'

But Nicole's primary concentration was still on her career. Her agent June Cairn, determined to keep her most gifted client's feet on the ground, advised her: 'Always remember you are a working actress. Not a star. If you become a star, fine. But at the moment you are a working actress.'

Nicole was asked in a TV interview: 'How are you going to handle it, years down the road, if you do become a big name and you are put on a pedestal?' 'Really badly,' she laughed. Then more seriously, she added: 'I can understand people becoming like hermits. I can really understand that. I think I would become more reclusive.'

The stage play *Steel Magnolias*, directed by Jon Ewing, provided a chance for Nicole to gain more experience in the theatre. At first she was excited about playing Shelby Estenton, one of the Southern belles who sit around at a hairdressing salon gossiping about men, marriage and the latest hairstyle. The play, 'in which the women tease each other more than their hair', appealed to her. 'It is an all-female cast. Men are central to the plot but being a play about women I felt secure in submerging myself in a role that could easily be related to . . . My character Shelby is a tough introduction to the rigours of live performance. She is on stage for the duration of the play and is a headstrong girl who is accustomed to getting her own way. It is a demanding role that should tell me whether or not this is the right path for me to take.'

But when the play opened in May at the York Theatre in Sydney, she was clearly concerned about appearing live on stage. 'I suppose I am something of a pessimist,' she said. 'I seem to look on the negative side of things too much. My dearest hope is for *Steel Magnolias* to be a smash hit but I do wonder whether or not my performance will be up to the standards of those around me. I know I have done enough in the past to look with reasonable confidence to the future but making a name for myself on the stage is important to me. These days it is important for any actor to be equally at home on television, film or theatre. You have to be versatile. Now I have overcome a fear of working in front of the cameras I have to get over the same fear of working in front of a live audience. It is a goal I have set for myself and I won't be happy until I've conquered it.'

Nicole learned a lot from working with stage stars like Nancye Hayes, Maggie Dence and Pat McDonald. She said she thought she was learning something new at every rehearsal.

The play was well reviewed and the Sydney *Morning Herald*

praised Nicole for 'making an impressive professional stage debut after her success in films'. She was nominated by the Sydney Theatre Critics Circle as the best newcomer.

Nicole celebrated her twenty-first birthday on 20 June 1988, during the run. Her co-stars made a fuss of her but boyfriend Tom Burlinson was away in London working on the TV mini-series *Piece of Cake* about Second World War fighter pilots and she decided to delay the big celebration until he was back from Britain.

But it was hardly worth waiting. The lovers had drifted apart, and by late summer 1988 'friends' were cheerfully informing the Australian media that the two-year romance between Tom Burlinson and Nicole Kidman was over. 'Tom wanted to settle down but Nicole was reluctant to make that commitment,' said one anonymous source. 'Nicole is very young and wants to consolidate her acting career.' Burlinson, who was still better known as *The Man from Snowy River*, sensibly said nothing. Nicole said: 'It's over now. We are still close. We always will be. He was my first love.'

By the time *Piece of Cake* went on television in Australia, Burlinson was sharing his life with fitness expert Adele Rankin and happy to confirm that he was still friendly with ex-lover Nicole. She could have done with a man around towards the end of 1988 because she was being plagued by a frightening stalker. She had let slip the location of her home in Sydney, 'And I had this crazy guy hanging around outside the house. It scared the hell out of me,' said Nicole. He pestered her for around six months. 'I was twenty-one and living alone in Sydney. A guy started following me. He would sit in the pub across the road and watch my every move. The first I knew about him was when friends said he had been asking questions.

They became suspicious because he pronounced by name Kideman instead of Kidman. But the police said they couldn't do anything until he attacked me! They talked to him but you never know how bad these people are going to be. There are always people whose behaviour defies description. I persuaded a few local cops to park their patrol car outside. That fixed him. I was lucky but it made me realise what other actresses suffer when they become the target of crazies.'

Handsome Australian actor Marcus Graham was best known down under for being the son of character actor Ron Graham and for starring as lovelorn landowner in the mini-series *Shadows of the Heart*. Until he fell in love with Nicole Kidman, that is. Then he was subjected to the spotlight of publicity throughout 1989. He was much closer to Nicole's age than Tom Burlinson – a year older than her, in fact. Marcus came from Perth and first worked mainly in theatre in productions such as *Biloxi Blues*, *The Rivers of China* and *Heartbreak Kid*. Then he was cast in *E Street* as Wheels the reclusive youngster bitter after being confined to a wheelchair after a motorcycle accident. 'The move into television was inevitable,' he said with great relief. 'I have been waiting to do it for some time. But some of these things I have been offered have been observed. Then there are others that simply haven't worked out.'

Marcus shared Nicole's lack of enthusiasm for talking pub-licly about their love affair, but gradually he began to open up. 'The more I establish myself,' said Marcus, 'the less I mind saying that Nicole and I are together. It was very hard, though, at the beginning. I felt our private life was being exposed for the whole world to see. I felt like people were stealing something from us and I don't like that. It is easier for Nicole to handle as she is more experienced and has already made it. For me, on the way up it is much harder. I first met Nic at the end of 1988 when she came to see me in the theatre in *Heartbreak Kid*. I then met her again in the foyer at the opening of something and asked her out.'

Nicole enjoyed dating Marcus, but she still chose to live alone to maintain her personal space and to give her the freedom her work requires. 'I never show my own personal emotions when I'm working. I save it for when I go home and I am by myself,' she said. 'But that is why I like living by myself, because it is you that's got to deal with it and you can't really lean on someone. You can't go and cry on a shoulder, you've got to come home to an empty house and you've got to be here with you and your mind.' While Kidman tackles everything with consummate professionalism she still had the enthusiasm and naïvety that is the trademark of a 21-year-old. 'I go out and see bands and movies. I play tennis and do aerobics and I've got friends that I see who are really important in my life,' she said. Whenever she was not busy acting she loved to travel and she loves to travel alone: 'Whenever I can I just take off for a couple of weeks. I have already been to America and Europe this year and my next stop is Russia. I love Italy and I am already learning Italian.'

Nicole starred as aspiring actress Mary McAllister in *The Bit Part*, a television movie screened in January 1989 on Channel Seven. It was written by Ian McFadyen from The Comedy Company and included lots of in-jokes about the TV and film business. The movie told the strange story of Mike Thornton, who quits his boring job as a school careers counsellor to become an actor.

Unfortunately the hapless Thornton discovers that acting is a job filled with inconvenient things such as auditions and having to accept lowly small roles just to pay the bills. It was a deeply forgettable movie apart from a terrific performance from Nicole as Mary McAllister, who has a fling with Thornton until, prophetically so far as Nicole was concerned, she realises life might be more interesting in Hollywood and promptly leaves. Mary spelled out her policy on stripping on screen: 'I don't object to nudity – just exploitative nudity.' And that was as funny as it got.

Emerald City opened in Australia in February 1989 just as Nicole signed up with top American agent Sam Cohn, the man who handled the careers of stars such as Meryl Streep. Nicole enthused about the wave of Australia-mania that seemed to be sweeping across the United States and was happy to be part of it. 'I've had a really good response over there,' she said. 'They are into Australian girls at the moment. They just find us very strange apparently. I suppose we are a bit rougher round the edges and a lot more laid back.'

In *Emerald City*, a strangely structured movie by David Williamson from his own stage play, Nicole was cast as Helen, the 'spunky young girlfriend' as the synopsis put it, of Sydney spiv Mike, played by Chris Haywood, an imaginative would-be media mogul whose ideas never seemed to quite get off the ground. Mike lured idealistic screenwriter Colin, played in what looked like a deep trance by John Hargreaves, into a sequence of improbable cooperations. Colin came from Melbourne, was swiftly seduced by the greed of his new partner, and almost by Helen as well. But, in spite of a passionate approach from Nicole, who brightened up the whole movie by refusing to allow her character to be merely a brainless bimbo, strangely he lost his nerve in one of the few compelling scenes in a disappointing film. The Australian's film critic Christine Cremen pointed out: 'Nicole Kidman scores a triumph. Of all the characters in *Emerald City* hers has the greatest potential, but sadly Williamson failed to realise it.' To be fair to Hargreaves he had the grace to praise Nicole afterwards: 'If I was an actress I would be really scared of her. She is going to get all the best roles.'

Kennedy–Miller announced the $5million mini-series, *Bangkok Hilton*, in March 1988. It was commissioned by the Ten Network and told the story of an Australian girl caught smuggling heroin in an Asian country. Terry Hayes leaked to the press that the series would be: 'A cross between a classic Hollywood melodrama and *Midnight Express*. We take a young girl from a stable family environment and she ends up in an Asian jail on Death Row and eventually escapes' thus giving away the ending even before production had begun. 'It is totally fictional but it is something that many people will be able to identify with.'

The six-hour mini-series written by Terry Hayes was in fact inspired by the terrible story of the murderous terrorist who kissed his pregnant Irish girlfriend goodbye as she boarded an aeroplane with his bomb in her bag, combined with the *Midnight Express* theme of an innocent person in a foreign jail. It became a brilliant vehicle for Nicole Kidman. Terry Hayes said: 'I wanted to write a script for Nicole Kidman. It would be the most demanding role an actress could imagine. It is the only thing I have ever written for an actor. I was so impressed by her in *Dead Calm*. I said I wanted to work with her again. She was alongside fine actors like Denholm Elliott and Norman Kaye. She is being challenged by working with fine actors and she is learning all the time.'

'It is a great role,' said Nicole with real enthusiasm about *Bangkok Hilton*. 'I may look terrible, with my hair pulled back and wearing all those dresses like sacks, but it is what acting is all about.' She was also attracted by the fact that it gave her the chance to work in exotic Goa on the west coast of India. 'My ambition is to have worked in every country. I don't believe in not having fun. That is why I like to travel. I think you have to live life to the full, otherwise you have nothing to draw on. That is my creed both as an actress and a person.'

Hayes tells the story of the horrendous duplicity of a handsome villain who seduces an innocent young girl in London and then tricks his innocent lover into carrying heroin through Thai customs for him. Jerome Ehlers plays a slimy drug dealer called Arkie Regan who seduces lonely Katrina, who is vainly searching for her father in London. Arkie charms Kat in England, romances her in India and finally dumps her in Thailand with 2.4kg of heroin which he has hidden in her camera case. She is caught, and is devastated by the betrayal. The penalty for drug smuggling is death. Thrown into jail, Kat is befriended by Mandy and her disabled brother Billy, who are then both cruelly executed by firing squad. She almost cracks under the grim conditions of her incarceration but finds deep wells of hidden strength and comes back fighting.

Nicole: 'The role was specially written for me so I felt insecure a lot of the time about how I was doing. Kat goes through culture shock at first and huddles in a corner. She is convinced she can't cope and then she finds strength from somewhere. It was very emotionally draining at times and at others very frustrating. It is not just a drug story. It is a story about unrequited love, betrayal, rejection, and a father and daughter who find each other.'

Nicole was happy to play a character who starts off as no great beauty. Kat was a very lonely plain Jane, a weedy and waif-like, deeply introverted figure. Plunged into a nightmare experience, she survived and emerged as a strong and confident woman. The big challenge for Nicole was that: 'Acting intro-verted and submissive is the very opposite to my own person-ality. That was the hardest thing for me to do in *Bangkok Hilton*. But, like anyone else, I can tap into my own feelings of betrayal and rejection in my own experience. It is like tapping into extremes of love and hate and loss, as I did in *Dead Calm*.' With her customary thoroughness, she researched the role by talking to a woman who had spent six years in a Thai jail, and insisted on wearing the heavy iron manacles in the jail scenes.

For months Nicole left her comfortable Sydney beachside apartment before dawn and drove to a grim former psychiatric hospital which served as the main location. She spent more than an hour in make-up having ugly bruises and mosquito bites painted on her willowy white body. 'It was not easy,' says Nicole with a shudder. 'The minute I arrived they got to work, putting dirt under my fingernails, oil in my hair and painted large dark circles under my eyes. It was emotionally very hard to work that way five days a week, twelve hours a day for eight weeks. It was so depressing but you can make that work for you.'

Nicole's drive and energy in even the most difficult conditions impressed everyone on the set: 'We did one very emotional scene and there were camera problems so we had to go back and do it again,' she said. 'It was very difficult. You couldn't just throw a tantrum, you just had to be very disciplined and do it again. People expect feature film quality from mini-series but you don't have the feature film's time or budget so it puts added pressures on everyone.' She added simply: 'These are dreadful conditions to work in with the dirt and the heat and the dust, but you have got to do the shot. I did *Dead Calm* in similar conditions to this. It was very hot and you always felt a bit sick. But you get used to not feeling one hundred per cent, to not feeling all that wonderful. You learn to cope because you know you have to do the shot. You have to make the decision whether to scream and carry on or just go ahead and do it. If you scream and carry on it is more stressful for everyone and that makes it so much harder. This business does not grind to a halt because of illness. You work even if you are at death's door. And the best thing is to have fun because if you can't enjoy what you're doing there is no reason to do it, is there?'

Life was more enjoyable for Nicole on location in Goa, where director Ken Cameron encouraged her and co-star Jerome Ehlers to relax into their more romantic scenes. An elderly grandmother selling mangoes wandered on to the speedily improvised set one morning and was instantly incorporated into the action. 'That is what makes Nicole such a professional and so wonderful to work with. She goes with the flow, staying in character. These location shots in Bangkok and India are the connective tissue. They will provide the realism and the colour.'

With the temperature at over 40 degrees and the high humidity, Nicole and Jerome spent a whole day capturing a single scene in which Arkie wakes his sunbathing lover with a kiss on an idyllic beach. 'This is the easy bit,' admitted Nicole. 'Sydney was heavy going. It was much more emotionally draining at home. I feel that I have been a bit lazy here. Usually when I am acting I feel more concentrated. I don't normally laugh and carry on between scenes. But here in this beautiful place, I feel much more relaxed.'

Nicole and her handsome co-star became firm friends and played many energetic tennis matches although she was more competitive than he was. Once he admitted defeat early by sticking a large sign that said No on his hotel room door. 'I have always been taught that you play to win,' said Nicole. 'I believe you should have drive and determination in whatever you do. You don't have to be ruthless but you have to be disciplined and drive yourself. That means sacrifices. The people who are successful are the ones who know what they want and go for it. I sometimes wonder where I will be in ten years. Will I be burned out? I try to fill my life with other things so that if it ends I won't keel over and die. But I would be upset. I think I would keep fighting. The most exciting careers are the ones that soar and plummet. I think it says something about the person.'

One night in Goa, Nicole led Jerome Ehlers in a fearless midnight swim in the Indian Ocean, ignoring the locals who were warning of the dangers of sea snakes. 'I've got a dangerous mentality,' says Nicole. 'I like the charge, the adrenaline pumping, the state of excitement. I put myself in fate's hands. If it is going to happen it's going to happen. I suppose in a way I tempt fate but it's the same with people who drive racing cars or jump out of aeroplanes. Acting provides one sort of excitement but I like to take risks as well.'

Ehlers's wife Emily was with him for some of the time and Nicole explained how she enjoys the way that a TV or film unit turns into an extended family. 'That is the great thing about working with people like this because everyone is in the same boat,' she said. 'You build up strong friendships and when you see the same people again in six months you feel that you have experienced something together. Australia is such a small country you tend to run into people again and again but I suppose that means you sort of drift in and out of their lives. Of course I get lonely and I really hate hotel rooms. The only thing I do in a hotel room is sleep and I will go out and do anything rather than stay in after that. It is a pet hate of mine. It doesn't matter if it is the most luxurious hotel room in the world, what do you do there apart from pick up the telephone? I don't have minders. I have to travel on my own a lot and do a lot of stuff by myself. But that is quite good because you learn to deal with yourself.'

The poverty of India left a searing impression on Nicole. On an overnight stay in the city of Bombay, every member of the cast and crew was affected by the pathetic, heart-rending sight of countless beggars scrabbling vainly for survival. Nicole found it a deeply upsetting and unnerving experience. She said afterwards: 'I was very depressed that night, I did not get any sleep. Seeing a place like that really increases your awareness, yet in another way I found I then became almost unemotional about it. I couldn't even cry. But it is good to be exposed to it.'

Nicole was well aware of the benefits of giving to charities that fought world poverty and was already a donor. Even before her visit to Bombay she had decided to do something else, something more personal. 'Just before I left Australia I began to sponsor a child in Kampuchea and when I saw some of the horrible sights in Bombay I thought, "Oh God, this is what it is all about." ' It was a shock to Nicole but afterwards she said she was glad she had experienced it. She wrote about it and her feelings in some detail in her diary. 'I write in my diary every night and I have been doing so since I was about eleven. It is fantastic. I can go back to the same date a year later and read what I was doing and how I was feeling. The way your priorities change is quite amazing.' But publishers around the world can refrain from dashing off a letter for the potential bestseller. Nicole says: 'And the best thing is that no one else will ever read my diaries. I am going to burn them all before I die.'

Bangkok Hilton director Ken Cameron quickly became a Nicole Kidman fan. He said: 'You are constantly surprised by the fact that one moment she seems to be a very young woman enjoying herself and being completely spontaneous. The next minute she is a serious actress, capable of a performance that can move you in a way that you don't expect from one so young. She looks wonderful, is enormously appealing on screen, and has something about her which belongs to the time. To have all those qualities is a rare thing.'

Nicole roared with laughter at being described as a combination of child and woman. 'Child,' she yelled. 'Hey, but I'm sophisticated.' Then more thoughtfully she added: 'Someone once told me that with acting you have to keep the child alive in you and that is very true. Sometimes you try to be adult and you have to have a certain amount of common sense, if that is what being an adult is. But you have got to keep the child alive.'

The enormously experienced director of photography on *Bangkok Hilton* was Geoff Burton, who had first worked with Nicole on *Vietnam*. The only time he had any difficulty was in making Nicole look plain and unappealing when she was incarcerated in the Bangkok jail. Burton said: 'Nicole has one of the easiest faces to photograph and it is really hard to make her look unattractive. Her great advantage is her hair which is very beautiful, light and radiant. No matter how it is dressed, it enhances her face so beautifully and creates its own frame. The camera caresses Nicole. If there is more than one person in the frame she is magnetic, she takes over. I knew in *Vietnam* there was something special about this girl and it has been fascinating to watch her develop. Nicole has this extraordinary confidence which, coupled with her intelligence, makes her unique as an actress. She is a star ascending. There is no doubt about it.' He had noted her talent and followed her progress and said: 'It is no longer in the hands of the agents, the manager or the publicists. Nicole is off and running and it doesn't matter what anyone does, it's all going to happen. The only thing which could go wrong is if she becomes personally affected in the process. I have seen it happen before and hopefully she will survive the pressure she will be under for the next five years. Nicole has an extremely strong base behind her, which I can only assume because she is so young, is her family. She has extraordinary confidence, beauty, diligence and intelligence and I'd say after the mini-series and the success of *Dead Calm* there is a good chance she will be lost to Australia. When you're that good you just can't stay at home.'

Nicole applies serious commitment to everything she does, whether it is in front of the camera or relaxing the Nicole Kidman way. On their one day off in Bangkok most of the cast and crew headed for the shops. But Nicole dragged co-star Jerome Ehlers to the other side of the city to an animal sanctuary to play with enormous pythons. On location in India after a gruelling day in the sun everyone headed to the bar to relax. Nicole had only a few drinks before retiring early to re-read scripts. She avoids late nights during a film shoot and admits to feeling guilty in Goa for laughing and joking in between takes.

Denholm Elliott played Kat's father. He was won over by the script: 'one of the best of its type that I have read'. Hal Stanton was the long-lost father who lives in self-imposed exile in Bangkok after being court-martialled as a Second World War traitor. He has to drag himself from his whisky bottle to help his daughter. Denholm saw similarities with his own character. 'I think I am like Stanton. I am a bit of an escapist and we both like a drink, though I think he could outdrink me easily. We have other things in common. He liked the Far East and I like the Far East, but he lived in a big house on the river in Bangkok without a mistress or a lover or anything and that is something I could never do. They'd be in and out like a fiddler's elbow if I lived there.' He took the part in *Bangkok Hilton* because of the eccentricities of the character. 'I'm an actor. It's like being a prostitute. You don't have to like the person, you just close your eyes and think of England.'

Denholm was deeply impressed by Nicole Kidman from the first moment they met. 'I thought Nicole was sensationally good. I think she is the new Vanessa Redgrave. I love to see somebody who has authority. They often have arrogance too, but she was sweet to work with. She is someone who has courage and taste and is not afraid to hold her ground and make her point and act with strength and vigour and passion. I think she should do a bit of work in the theatre, it would help her movements and her voice. It would help everybody to work out of the theatre when you are that age. It gives you an authority and an ease of movement. The trouble is that people go to the top through television and become great

Daddy's little girl: Nicole with her father Antony

The Kidman family: Nicole with her sister Antonia, mother Janelle and father Antony

Pedal power: biking after baddies in teen movie BMX *Bandits*

Handsome actor Tom
Burlinson was Nicole's
first love

Actor Marcus Graham
fell for Nicole after
meeting her in 1988

Fighting for dear life with Billy Zane in the chilling movie *Dead Calm*

In long blonde wig as a snooty schoolgirl with Thandie Newton in *Flirting*

Doubling up: Nicole and Tom Cruise teamed up on screen in *Days of Thunder* (above) and *Far and Away* (below)

Playing moll to Dustin Hoffman's gangster in *Billy Bathgate*

Plotting evil with Alec Baldwin in *Malice*

Brazen as ambitious
weather girl Suzanne
Stone in *To Die For*

Helplessly trapped by
John Malkovich in
The Portrait of a Lady

Snuggling up to husband Tom Cruise in happier times

international stars and they never do their basic homework. It's like trying to play the piano without learning your scales. Nicole was a joy to work with from start to finish. She not only takes the work deadly seriously, and that is important, but can always turn up the brilliance when she has to.'

Nicole was equally impressed with the veteran English character actor. She told friends that Denholm was one of the funniest men she had ever met. She expected some traditional English reserve but found an old rascal who could not resist telling her his favourite tall tales. 'Denholm was wonderful,' she said. 'He was always full of good stories about people like Woody Allen and never ceased to make us laugh.'

The final episode of *Bangkok Hilton* went out on Channel 10 on 7 November 1989, and the decade ended with Nicole heading for Hollywood. Before she left she told the Sydney *Daily Mirror*: 'I was thirteen in 1980, which is about when I began working as an actress. I have grown up in a decade that did not promise a great future. But we did not grow up like our mothers, expecting to get married, have children and everything would be all right. Life just isn't going to be like that. I am the daughter of academic parents who taught me to question everything and not to "go around with stars in my eyes". Father a source of strength and mother a source of inspiration. At home I have always been taught to demand a lot of myself and I think that stands you in good stead. I went to an all-girls' school, North Sydney Girls' High, which was very career oriented and success oriented. The atmosphere was competitive. It encouraged us all to be ambitious and I don't think that is a bad thing.'

In the eighties Katharine Hepburn was Nicole's idol. 'She's an extraordinary woman who refuses to conform and lives life the way she wants. I bought an old picture of her once and asked her to autograph it, but she wouldn't. She doesn't do autographs. I'd love to make a movie as an ode to her. I just need to find someone good enough to write it.' Katharine Hepburn was also very tall and when she pointed out to Spencer Tracy that she was taller than him, he said in a remark which amuses Nicole: 'Don't worry I'll cut you down to size.' Cruise's shortness never bothered her, and she liked the way he refused to be inhibited by it.

Nicole admired Katharine Hepburn: 'Because she is a survivor. She is independent, a bit of a rebel and she has always stuck to her guns. I admire Jane Fonda because she has had an incredible life and still kept searching for more. I admire Margaret Thatcher as a woman, not for her politics. And I admire Benazir Bhutto for getting where she has. I admire Australian film producers Pat Lovell and Margaret Fink for making beautiful films at a time when it was very difficult for women to get into the industry.'

Among her other heroines are Ingrid Bergman, Vanessa Redgrave, Ava Gardner – all women who live their lives, who are not afraid of the consequences of their actions. 'Because they all rebelled against what others wanted to slot them into. They were women with a cause. I think what Fonda did in the sixties was wonderful, how she stood up and defied her country and said how terrible the Vietnam war was.'

Nicole was fascinated by the sixties and was anxious to make a controversial film. She immersed herself in movies: 'I think Al Pacino in *Dog Day Afternoon* is incredible', and she read widely from *War and Peace* to a biography of Meryl Streep.

For the nineties Nicole shared the concern of many of her generation over the environment and nuclear disarmament. 'We all have to take a strong look at the kind of people who are leading our country. We have to become much more politically aware. It is important to read and to be informed, not just glance at the newspapers and say, "Oh well." In the nineties and into the twenty-first century it is saving our environment that will matter most. I also think health issues are important ones. It is tough enough for young women to form relationships because of diseases like AIDS. Health fears mean women do not want to leave boyfriends they have had for some time. We are getting back to the situation where women marry early and have kids and I think that is dangerous. Marriage is not a big issue with me. It is finding someone who is supporting, loving and concerned that matters and I think that is very hard. Life is short. You do not have much time so you must follow your own star. That may sound selfish but it is not meant to be. It is just what my mother always said to me: "Whatever you do in life don't give up on your dreams." '

In Australia *Bangkok Hilton* achieved the highest ratings for a mini-series for six years. It broke ratings records, with a top McNair Anderson Sydney viewers' figure of 40 points – 41 in Melbourne – for the last episode. It became one of the highest-rated Australian television series ever screened. Channel 10 was over the moon even though the Australian Film Industry Awards controversially ignored Nicole, who was not even nominated as best actress in a mini-series, an award most viewers believed she deserved.

The show was a hit all over the world. In Britain the BBC were delighted with the ratings it achieved and in the United

States the critics praised Nicole's performance as 'excellent' and acclaimed her as a charismatic and compelling actress. But as the champagne corks popped, Nicole was the only person not able to join in the celebrations. She was sitting at home quietly trying to fend off a sudden bout of tonsillitis. 'It is fantastic that so many people watched *Bangkok Hilton*,' she croaked. 'I just feel too ill to celebrate.'

Nicole Kidman's last Kennedy–Miller production before she hit Hollywood was *Flirting*. The sequel to Duigan's hit film *The Year My Voice Broke*, *Flirting* charted the romance between a boarding school pupil, played by Noah Taylor, and a beautiful Ugandan girl from a neighbouring school, played by Thandie Newton. It was written and directed by John Duigan whose work Nicole loves. 'Nicole plays a very bossy school prefect,' says George Miller. 'She is a bit of a bad guy. She is very snooty in this role. Not at all like she is in real life. I think Nicole has given some of her best performances for John Duigan. When he wrote *Flirting* he thought it would be interesting to cast Nicole in this role. He knows her range, he sees what she is capable of.'

Nicole tucked her hair underneath a blonde wig and climbed into a very sexy-looking school uniform and said: 'I will be playing every schoolboy's fantasy – and the schoolgirl the other girls love to hate. It is my last chance to be a schoolgirl.' She was terrific as overbearing Nicola Radcliffe and was delighted to play a relatively minor character as a favour to Duigan. 'I was told that I looked like Fergie,' said Nicole. 'A cross between Fergie and Sigourney – that baffled me. They want to link you to all these different people. I suppose that is how I get typecast. I get told I can play a strong female, for example, when I would like to play a shattered female.' The movie won prizes at the Australian Film Industry Awards ceremony for best film, the AFI Members' Prize, and prizes for production, design and editing before it opened in Australia in March 1991.

Nicole's one regret as she prepared to leave her native land was being parted from her family, but she knew that wherever she went they would always be there for her. 'My parents have always thought acting was a great way of developing the imagination and growing as a person. But when anything went wrong they would say to me, "Well, you can always go to university." As an actor you tend to be either at huge heights of happiness or in the depths of depression. Anyway I do, I don't know about other actors. I would ring in a panic from, say London, about something and my parents' stock answer would be, "Oh well, you can always go to university." Then you think there are other options. But this is what I want to do, so I am willing to work hard at it. My parents are very level-headed people who have nothing to do with the industry. They are very supportive, very. The best parents you could ever hope for. They have pushed me, yes, but they have never forced their attitudes on me.'

CHAPTER 6

Thunder in Florida

'Any girl that can stand up and walk out on Warren Beatty because she doesn't think he's serious about offering her a part, is pretty serious about her career'

– TERRY HAYES

I f Tom Cruise had quickly fallen under Nicole Kidman's spell after seeing her in *Dead Calm* and then meeting her in the flesh, then he was not the only Hollywood leading man to do so. Legendary lothario Warren Beatty, who had romanced some of Hollywood's most famous women, was also much taken by the beauty and the acting ability of the young girl he had seen in *Dead Calm*.

Beatty, famed as an actor and producer as well as for the way women fell for his good looks, sex appeal, charm and renowned prowess as a lover, soon got in touch with Nicole while she was over in Los Angeles and invited her to come and see him. They met, talked about movies, Hollywood, Nicole's aims and ambitions and Beatty's own upcoming projects, and he gave her plenty of useful advice about the movie industry.

As an experienced producer and actor, Beatty was naturally a fascinating man for her to meet and to get to know. She did not delude herself that she was the first starlet to whom Beatty was happy to pass on his knowledge of the machinations of Tinseltown, but she nevertheless lent a willing ear to what he had to say.

The raw young actress and the seasoned Hollywood idol, fully thirty years older than her and the sensational star of *Bonnie and Clyde* the year before Nicole was born, met up several times. He found her every bit as gorgeous as he had expected after seeing *Dead Calm*, stimulating company and very desirable. According to Terry Hayes, at one of their early meetings Warren turned on the famous Beatty charm full beam. Holding up his hands in front of his eyes as if he was being blinded by a bright light, he said to Nicole: 'I can't stand it, I can't stand it . . . being in a room with such beauty. You must have dinner with me.' Nicole politely refused. Hundreds of beautiful girls would have grabbed the chance to have dinner with Beatty and enjoyed being intoxicated by his potent, masculine charisma. But Nicole was not interested in a dinner date with Beatty. She was not about to become his latest sexual conquest.

Picking up the story, Hayes recalled: 'I think there were four meetings and at every one Nicole refused to have dinner. It was on the last meeting that Warren walked Nicole to her car and again asked her to have dinner with him, this time on bended knee. Nicole said to him: "Oh get up, Warren!" '

Hayes, who always felt thoroughly protective of Nicole, said that her response to such an overture by one of the world's great lovers indicated to him that she would be more than capable of holding her own and her head up high in the harsh Hollywood jungle. 'That's when I knew she was going to be OK,' he said with relief.

A chuckling Hayes later topped off the story of the encounter when speaking glowingly about Nicole on national television in Australia for a TV portrait of the actress for the much respected documentary programme *60 minutes*. 'Any girl,' he said, 'that can stand up and walk out on Warren Beatty because she doesn't think he's serious about offering her a part, is pretty serious about her career.' Beatty did, however, lend a helping hand by showing Nicole's screen test to screenwriter Robert Towne.

Nicole's first experience of the serious business of movie making, Hollywood style, was by now just months away. *Days of Thunder*'s writer Robert Towne accommodated the creation of Nicole's character Dr Claire Lewicki into the revised script for the film and promised her she would not 'get lost in the shuffle'. It was a part tailored to fit Nicole's background. She would be a young Australian resident neurologist at the Daytona Beach Hospital who treats Tom Cruise's injured racing driver character Cole Trickle and falls in love with him.

The movie had sprung from Tom Cruise's burgeoning interest in motor racing. Paul Newman, with whom Cruise had starred in *The Color of Money*, was a devoted racing fan and much of his enthusiasm for the sport had rubbed off on Tom. Newman had even encouraged Tom to enrol for a one-day seminar at a Georgia racetrack where track officials were impressed by his efforts behind the wheel. Newman was also able to regale Tom with stories about the 1969 movie *Winning* in which he had starred as an ace racing driver. But, apart from *Grand Prix*, starring James Garner back in 1967, the world of movies had rarely done full justice to the world of motor racing. Tom felt it was high time it did.

A few years earlier Tom had experienced the high-speed thrill of a few laps round Daytona, possibly the most famous racetrack in the world, and was immediately smitten not only by the experience but by the dedication and the level of commitment shown by the race car fraternity at high levels of competition. He decided there and then he must make a movie about a driver and the business of motor racing.

Tom's mounting obsession with racing neatly coincided with *Top Gun* producers Don Simpson and Jerry Bruckheimer pressing him to star in a sequel to their aerobatic blockbuster. Reluctant to reprise his pilot's role, Tom saw *Days of Thunder*, however, as a perfect follow-up with the two producers. Conversely, they could clearly see it could be a *Top Gun* on wheels. If Tom was not going to strap on his air combat helmet for them once more, then Tom at speed inside a racing driver's crash helmet might be a terrific substitute and a winner at the box office. With a healthy budget estimated at $30 million and such a strong production pedigree, *Days of Thunder* had everything going for it to be a commercial success.

There would be many weeks of filming before Nicole would be needed but, from the start there was a pressured schedule for the movie because Paramount decided they wanted it ready for release in the autumn of 1990.

When Nicole arrived to join the set at Daytona Beach, Florida, in the latter part of 1989, she found she had a lot of hanging around and waiting to do while Tom was in almost every scene. She was impressed with the long hours he was prepared to put in, his energy and his dedication. 'I thought Tom was an incredible man, totally self-confident about who he was and what he wanted, the kind of person who inspires confidence right off the bat,' she said. But it was some time before a friendship flowered. Watching him from a distance, she at first just exchanged the odd smile with him. He had, she could not help but notice once again, a beautiful smile.

Shooting was halfway over by the time they had their first scenes together. Nicole found Tom cool and giving as an actor and not afraid to open up and show his emotions. 'One of the first things I thought when I met him was that he was a nice guy,' she said. Gradually the couple got to know each other and Nicole later admitted: 'We clicked. We made each other laugh.'

Tom was amused that Nicole did not know one end of a car from another and even had some difficulty over a scene in which her character had to drive an automatic BMW. At home in Australia, she explained to him, she drove her mum's old VW. Nicole had certainly never seen a motor race in her life and he therefore could not help admiring her spirit when she jumped at his offer to take her for a spin with him round the Daytona track in the supercharged car he drove in the film. As he pressed the accelerator ever closer to the floor and the speedometer needle touched a breathtaking 180 miles an hour, he was surprised to hear his passenger yelling in his ear over the roar of the engine: 'Faster! Faster! Faster!' Nicole wound up with a sore neck from having her head jerked back as Tom took the car zooming through the gears. But, she said with obvious excitement, it got her adrenaline pumping. Tom was impressed with this unexpected spark of vitality. He was elated she was so exhilarated by the high-speed ride he had given her. This girl has a delightfully audacious streak, he told close associates on the set. It was a first taste of the adventurous lifestyle they would pursue together in years to come.

Before long Tom was starting to look at his screen love interest in a new light and either his white rented BMW or his Harley Davidson motorcycle could be spotted parked outside the Daytona Beach condominium where Nicole was based for the film shoot. But Tom was a married man with an actress wife, Mimi Rogers, back at their luxurious home in Brentwood, Los Angeles. His growing friendship with Nicole, therefore, led to much tabloid newspaper gossip and prompted paparazzi to stake out Nicole's apartment. Eventually she found herself on the front cover of America's prestigious *People* magazine with only her mane of red hair visible as she and Tom roared off on his motorcycle.

Tom denied any romantic involvement with Nicole, whom he described as just a friend and acting colleague. To the persistent probing questions from the tabloids, Nicole said, with her tongue very firmly in her cheek, 'I do get lonely when I'm on the road, especially when I don't have anyone to get into bed with and watch the telly.'

But the truth was that Tom's marriage was in trouble. He had married Mimi, who was some seven years older than him, on 9 May 1987, in great secrecy after first setting eyes on her at a Los Angeles dinner party. Mimi was then dating someone else and more than a year passed before they bumped into each other again and found they immediately clicked.

To most observers their three-year marriage seemed solid enough by the time Tom embarked on filming *Days of Thunder* but they had begun having marital problems. On more than one occasion towards the end of 1989, Tom had briefly moved out of their house as they tried to sort out their difficulties.

As his friendship with Nicole began to develop, Tom felt pangs of guilt, although there is absolutely no suggestion that the couple began a physical affair until much later on. In early December Mimi flew to Florida to join Tom during the filming of *Days of Thunder*. But if she had hopes of saving their marriage, they were soon to be dashed. Not long after her arrival, Tom asked for a divorce and told the shattered Mimi: 'I'm with Nicole now.' Realising there was little point in trying to talk Tom round, Mimi flew back to Los Angeles distraught. Tom's lawyers were soon in touch with her to work out a deal that would be as painless for them both as possible, and kept secret.

While the rumours continued to gather pace around the set and the gossip about Tom and Nicole intensified, the two stars kept a respectable distance, even at a New Year's Eve party funded by Tom for the *Days of Thunder* cast and crew in Charlotte, North Carolina.

Less than a fortnight later Mimi Rogers made one last but fruitless effort to save her marriage, arriving in Charlotte to meet up with Tom on 11 January at the Charlotte Hilton-University Place hotel.

But it was of no avail. Five days later divorce papers with 'Thomas Cruise' as the petitioner and 'Miriam Cruise, aka Mimi Rogers Cruise the respondent' were filed on 16 January at Los Angeles County's Superior Court of California. Tom had personally signed the petition on 12 January, the day after Mimi's last-ditch meeting with him. The petition was for a dissolution of the marriage citing 'irreconcilable differences'. The date of actual separation was given as 9 December 1989. The divorce was to become final during the last weeks of shooting *Days of Thunder*.

The announcement of the separation hit the headlines around the world the following day, on 17 January. Confirming the split, the couple said there had been some 'very positive aspects' to the marriage but there were also 'some issues which could not be resolved'.

Caught up in the maelstrom of Tom's marital upheaval, Nicole just got on with her role and she was pleased for her co-star when Tom not only made the front page of much respected *Time* magazine for his latest movie, *Born on the Fourth of July*, but also, on 22 January, won a Golden Globe Best Actor award for his role in the film as a wheelchair-bound Vietnam veteran.

As the weeks gave way to months, Nicole and Tom were gradually able to display their growing feelings for each other more openly, often dining out together at the Olive Garden restaurant at Daytona Beach and being spotted strolling hand in hand. When asked about Tom, Nicole could now be supportive but would not discuss wedding plans. 'Tom has gone through a hard time in his personal life and at these moments friends should support each other,' she said loyally.

The confirmation that they were now very much a couple came at the 1990 Oscars, where Tom was again up for a Best Actor award for *Born on the Fourth of July*. He had let it be known that he intended to take his mother, Mary Mapother, to the ceremony as his date. But when his white stretch limousine drew up outside the Dorothy Chandler Pavilion in Los Angeles, Tom emerged with his mother on his right arm and Nicole on his left. Nicole looked radiantly beautiful in a simple black dress and high, high heels.

Their limousine was one of the last to arrive. Tom and Nicole had hoped that by then most of the reporters, photographers and television crews would have scurried inside anxious not to miss a moment of the awards ceremony. But there was still a formidable contingent waiting for them.

There were gasps from the assembled crowd as it dawned on them that Tom was with Nicole. This was Tom's first official public appearance with another woman since he had announced his marriage split from Mimi Rogers. The fact that he and Nicole were showing up together on Hollywood's biggest night of the year seemed to demonstrate to observers that the couple were ratifying all the stories that they were an item. The presence of Tom's mother also seemed to show that she was welcoming Nicole as the new love in her son's life and indicating her approval.

Their arrival prompted journalists and TV men to surge forward, all eagerly scrambling to quiz the couple about this development. But Tom stayed silent and Nicole ignored the microphones thrust her way, smiled brightly and moved swiftly inside with Tom and Mary. Together they took their seats next to Tom's good friend and *Rain Man* co-star, Dustin Hoffman. They had been placed in the front row of the auditorium – two glamorous stars who would now be seen as a couple by billions on television sets around the world.

With Nicole by his side, Tom had hoped this would prove to be his proudest moment, but he failed to repeat his Golden Globe success. He did, however, seem genuinely pleased for British actor Daniel Day-Lewis who won the Oscar for his role in *My Left Foot*. After the awards ceremony, Tom and Nicole shunned the many celebrity parties to which they had been invited and instead headed for the luxury L'Hermitage Hotel in Beverly Hills where Tom had booked suite 705 for a private party for seventy friends – with the media very definitely excluded. Next morning he and Nicole boarded a private jet and were flown back to Florida for further filming on *Days of Thunder*. Although Tom had not triumphed, it had still been quite a night for the couple. Nicole had declined to go to the Oscars ceremony when Tom first asked her. Then she thought: why not? Now she was glad she had gone.

It had been an exciting experience and she was glad to support Tom and offer sympathy when he did not win. She told him he did not need a gold statuette on the mantelpiece because he had the lasting legacy of the film itself. It was the movie that was gold, and in twenty years' time his children would sit down and watch it. One important aspect of the Oscars registered strongly with Nicole. 'You realise when you're sitting there that this isn't what you do it for – and that is must never, ever be a driving motivation.'

Nicole would not have been the first young actress to embark on an affair with her leading man during the making of a movie. On-set affairs are commonplace, but many turn out to be strictly location affairs for the duration of filming and the relationships cease after the cameras have finished creating fantasy, as cast and crew scatter in different directions back to the real world.

But it eventually became apparent that Nicole and Tom were not having an on-set fling. They were very much in love. 'I've never been affected by anyone to that degree,' Nicole was to explain years later. 'It was very scary because you know that there's almost no going back.'

During the filming, Nicole was regularly on the phone to her mother keeping her informed of developments, not least of her blossoming friendship with Tom. Inevitably there were times when she desperately missed her home and family in Sydney and her mother tried to help her by sending out 'care packages' of Australian newspapers and magazines as well as jars of

Vegemite, the spread so beloved of Australians.

Eventually Janelle flew out to Florida to visit her daughter and to meet Tom for the first time. They appeared to get on fine, certainly well enough for Janelle to reveal in time that she enjoyed playing Scrabble with him and a game of charades, although she did note how competitive he was. She was later quoted as saying he was 'an intense, energetic 27-year-old with a great sense of humour and a very nice way of throwing his head backwards when he laughs'.

Janelle stayed with Nicole for a fortnight in Florida and they were thrilled to see each other, to have time for a good gossip over an early morning cup of tea, and to do exciting things together – even going canoeing. At Tom's urging, mother and daughter went to the cinema one afternoon to see *Born on the Fourth of July*. He was prouder of this movie than of any other he had been in.

Born on the Fourth of July was based on the true story of crippled ex-US Marine Sgt Ron Kovic of Massapequa, Long Island. Born on 4 July, American Independence Day, Kovic had grown up as a god-fearing, very respectable, upstanding young man whose heroes had been John Wayne and President John F. Kennedy. When Kovic received the call-up for Vietnam, he was proud to go off to serve his country believing that to be his duty as an American man. In Vietnam, however, things go terribly wrong. He accidentally kills a fellow marine in battle and returns to his homeland in a wheelchair after being wounded in action. Ahead of him is the prospect of spending the rest of his life crippled and impotent.

Born on the Fourth of July was directed by Oliver Stone, the same Oliver Stone who had given cinemagoers eye-blistering images in a savage yet moving account of a nineteen-year-old soldier's baptism under fire in Vietnam in his previous film, *Platoon*. With his astute handling of Kovic's story in *Born on the Fourth of July*, Stone once again showed America to itself in a way it was not going to forget and won himself a Best Director Oscar in the process.

He drenched the film in visceral reality and coaxed a stunning performance from Tom Cruise who spent weeks in a wheelchair alongside Kovic in preparation for the movie and forged a strong friendship with the Vietnam veteran. After a string of highly commercial movies, Tom received terrific praise from all quarters for the way he depicted Kovic's odyssey from true believer to wheelchair-bound disenchantment, from eager, pure-hearted teen to long-haired activist. The film had shown Tom Cruise possessed an unexpected versatility as an actor.

Janelle found herself shedding tears as she watched *Born on the Fourth of July*, especially during the scene in which the young Ron Kovic runs through the rain to see his girlfriend at the prom just before he leaves for Vietnam where his beliefs and his life will be shattered. In the cinema seat next to her, Nicole too was misty-eyed and moved by the depth of Tom's perform-ance. It was after seeing him in that movie, she said, that she really fell in love with him.

When news of Tom's split from Mimi Rogers came out into the open, the *Days of Thunder* crew noticed that some of the tension in Tom that had been so evident during filming now seemed to fall away. Quite clearly Nicole's presence had much to do with this, and while she was being swept off her feet by the number one box-office star, he for his part was starting to discover ever more qualities he liked about the Australian actress, not least her adventurous streak. She certainly liked a challenge, he noted.

Tom was pleasantly surprised when Nicole readily agreed to join him for a spot of sky diving, a hobby he regularly liked to pursue. When Nicole was sixteen she had tried to persuade her parents to let her jump out of a plane but they refused to sign the consent forms out of concern for her safety. She had often dreamed of what it would be like to free fall with nothing but space around her. Now, at Tom's invitation, she had the perfect opportunity to make a free fall parachute jump and she was not going to miss out this time.

It was an experience Nicole would never forget. Her heart was pumping and she could scarcely breathe as she stood ready to throw herself out of the plane. The wind buffeting her face felt ice cold. She was shaking and laughing at the same time and remembers: 'That first jump you think "Oh my God, oh my God, I'm going to die." And then you're out there and it's not like floating. You're dropping through the air at 180 miles an hour and all the skin on your face is pushed back and it's like whooosh, and then you pull the parachute and you're floating.'

Back safely on terra firma after that first jump, an adrenaline-charged Nicole was shaking with excitement while Tom was full of admiration for her. 'You've got guts, honey,' he told her. He also thought it was pretty cool that a girl was happy to throw herself out of a plane with him. Nicole could not wait to get back up in the air and do it all over again. It was her turn to think Tom was pretty cool when in mid-air, as they plunged towards the earth, he was able to manoeuvre himself towards her and plant a quick kiss on her lips. 'It wasn't a long, passionate kiss – more of a peck, really,' she explained. The brief embrace as they parachuted to the ground could hardly have been more symbolic – they were a high-flying couple madly in love.

It was during the filming of *Days of Thunder* that it fully dawned on Nicole how big a part Tom had played in securing the role of Dr Claire Lewicki for her. Ultimately she was to declare that the role was 'unsatisfying', but at the time she saw it as an entrée to Hollywood, a chance to widen her horizons and a stepping stone to bigger things. 'It was Tom who really pushed hard for me to be taken on,' she said. 'He wanted me to play opposite him, to be the girl who falls for the hero in the storyline. He played a big part in getting that written into the script especially for me – he had it created for me.'

Naturally Tom and Nicole's love scenes in the film crackled on screen, passionate enough for producer Don Simpson to promise American movie fans: 'You'll see Tom and Nicole in all their hormonal glory.' The couple's real-life love affair added spice to the movie and it was even decided that the couple should shoot an additional love scene in a thinly veiled effort to cash in on it.

The extra scene was a tight squeeze in every sense because time was pressing. Inclement weather had already hampered the shooting of the racing scenes and now Paramount had made the decision to bring forward the film's release date to the 4 July holiday weekend of 1990 which left director Tony Scott with precious little editing time.

In the circumstances, Scott made a good job of *Days of Thunder*, his direction taking cinema audiences into the maelstrom of stock car racing with an effective blend of car-mounted camera-work and long lenses lending documentary credibility and impact. The roar of the engines and the high-speed theme incorporated elements of the *Top Gun* blockbuster.

The story unfolded with Randy Quaid as Tim Daland, the owner of a used car dealership, dreaming of making his name on the stock car circuit. He persuades a racing veteran, Harry Hogge, played by Robert Duvall, to build him a competitive car provided that he, Daland, finds a suitable driver. Enter Tom Cruise, as Cole Trickle, on a motorcycle, a young man who is unsuitable in every way. But he has a thirst for speed, is desperate to drive and proves himself no slouch behind the wheel. He is also fiercely competitive. After an indifferent start, Trickle begins to prove he is a winner but finds himself rivalling champion Rowdy Burns, played by Michael Rooker, an old hand whose dream is to get out of racing with his mind and body intact and to work on the farm he has purchased for his family. When Trickle has an accident which almost kills him, he winds up at the same hospital as Burns under the attention of Nicole as Dr Claire Lewicki. Her loving care, which blossoms into an affair, aids Trickle's recovery, but when he returns to the track he discovers he has lost his edge.

Tom played the strangely named Trickle as a cocky but insecure young challenger trying to break into the big time and out to unseat Rooker as the champion. Randy Quaid competently played the crass promoter, and Robert Duvall came out of the movie in a healthy light for his role as the manager who coaches an untrusting Cruise by radio from trackside.

After such a formidable performance in a leading role in *Dead Calm*, Nicole had little to do other than look sexy in *Days of Thunder*. When the movie came out, she was, however, irritated that so many people seemed to think her character Claire was a neurosurgeon. 'I wasn't a neurosurgeon,' she corrected one interviewer. 'I was an intern, which means I'm just a medical student. I get everybody on that.'

The reviews for the movie were disappointing, although it went on to take a reported $80 million at the box office. 'It's actually the most successful racing movie in the history of film,' Cruise pointed out to one interviewer who dared to suggest *Days of Thunder* was a bit of a flop critically and only a moderate commercial success.

At least *Days of Thunder* was a foot in the Hollywood door for her, and Tony Scott reckoned Nicole could become the first Australian actress to make it big internationally. 'I keep forgetting how young she is,' he said. 'Just keep watching her.'

At the time the *Days of Thunder* experience seemed like a fairytale to Nicole: little-known Australian actress goes to America, has a part specially created for her in a multi-million-dollar movie, and the biggest star in Hollywood falls head over heels in love with her. It seemed to be the predestined happy ending when she went on to become Mrs Cruise.

CHAPTER 7

✳

Colorado Confetti

'I'd like to get married one day, but I think it would be very foolish to do so at this stage of my life when there are so many other things I want to do. It annoys me when people make this assumption that when you meet a wonderful man, you want to drop everything and marry him'
— NICOLE KIDMAN

In the months after completing *Days of Thunder*, Tom and Nicole at last had the chance to get to know each other properly. Nicole made it plain that she was not going to compromise her lifestyle just because she was with a famous movie star who was recognised and mobbed wherever he went. She was determined they should try to go about their lives as any normal couple would. She was not going to stay inside just to avoid the fans. And one of the first things she insisted on was that Tom should get rid of his chauffeur. Tom enjoyed driving (she did not) so it made sense that he should sit behind the wheel enjoying her company rather than have the potential intrusion and encumbrance of a chauffeur. Both were happy to take off somewhere at a whim and Nicole wanted it to be just the two of them.

Together they embarked on a leisurely drive across California, just as an ordinary couple, with no phones, no agents and no entourage to disturb them. Tom took Nicole to the desert in Palm Springs and there, on a lonely stretch of road, he taught her how to ride a motorbike.

They also took off to the Bahamas for a holiday and went scuba diving. Once she had got over the claustrophobia, Nicole warmed to undersea adventures swimming with sting-rays and moray eels. Scuba diving was added to her list of athletic pursuits.

The couple had just a week in the Bahamas but made the most of it, going for leisurely walks, cooking meals on the sand, sleeping in hammocks and talking about their respective fami-lies and backgrounds, their interests, likes and dislikes. She and Tom, Nicole decided, were kindred spirits. They both had nomadic, gypsy natures, and when it came to outdoor pursuits they were both thrill-seekers who loved a sniff of danger. Nicole was deliriously happy with her ultra-famous lover and the life they were now enjoying. She kept telling Tom how lucky she was to have him in her life. No, he kept repeating to her, he felt he was the lucky one. 'You're just enough of a gentleman,' she would tell him, referring to the potent mixture of charm and virility she found so exciting.

Nicole was not a mercenary soul and money had never been her motivation for wanting an acting career. But Tom Cruise, who was by now commanding around $10 million a movie, was able to offer her a lifestyle beyond the wildest dreams of any girl of Nicole's age. After dating actor boyfriends who, like her, would sometimes wonder where the next job, and therefore the next meal, was coming from, she would not have been human if she had not been swayed by the kind of luxurious lifestyle Cruise was able to offer her. He was then reputed to be worth an estimated $25 million, he travelled by private jet, stayed at the most exclusive hotels, and when he socialised it was with a tight-knit circle of friends which included Dustin Hoffman and Paul Newman.

Not long after the world had officially learned that they were a couple, Tom splashed out around $5 million on a magnificent colonial-style home for himself and Nicole in an acre of land in Pacific Palisades, a highly sought after area west of Los Angeles. Imposingly situated behind electric gates, the 1940s two-storey house comprised five bedrooms and five bathrooms, a wood-panelled library and a spectacular spiral staircase leading to the upper floor. Outside, there was a two-storey guest house, a swimming pool and spa, and an English garden. It was a fabulous home even by Hollywood standards but Tom spared no expense in having it transformed into a palace for the new love of his life. Gradually a cinema was added, plus a snooker room and a Jacuzzi and Tom eventually added an Australian touch – a gum tree in the garden to remind Nicole of home. The garden was a special joy to Nicole who tended the vegetable patch herself. With a lot of shrubbery and trees around the house, she liked to think of it as their oasis in the middle of LA.

On Thursday 9 August 1990 Nicole Kidman and Tom Cruise flew by private jet into Sydney for their first trip to Australia together. They were met by Janelle Kidman, and were whisked away from the airport in a beige Commodore – in such a rush to avoid the press that they sped away with the boot of the car still gaping open and had to stop to close it.

While they checked into a luxury suite at the Sebel Town-house, there was feverish press speculation that the couple had flown in to tell Nicole's family of their plans to marry. But the couple simply grinned and would not comment on the subject when questioned by the press pack who swarmed round them as Nicole showed Tom around Sydney.

Nicole's position on the matter became quite clear when she met up with writer Simon Kinnersley, and she also took the opportunity to shoot down stories that Tom had been lavishing gifts upon her. 'All that talk about us being engaged is just nonsense,' she confided to Simon. 'There is no ring, engage-ment or otherwise. Nor have there been any earrings. And while we are at it, in spite of the stories about Tom winning my heart by sending me a dozen red roses every day for weeks, I'm afraid I need a little more than that. I don't know any woman who fell for a man because of a few roses. Besides Tom has a lot more to offer than just that.'

Nicole admitted that she and Tom were very much in love, but she did not think Tom was in any rush to get married for a while. 'And I think I'm far too young,' she added. 'I'd like to get married one day, but I think it would be very foolish to do so at this stage of my life when there are so many other things I want to do. It annoys me when people make this assumption that when you meet a wonderful man you want to drop everything and marry him. I wouldn't turn down work in the interests of a relationship or to try to save it. I'm very serious about my work and how far I want it to go.'

In Sydney the couple had lunch with Terry Hayes and George Miller at a smart brasserie before going walkabout in the King's Cross area, hotly pursued by cameramen. Tom went up a few notches in everyone's estimation when he stopped to help to his feet a photographer who had been sent crashing to the ground in the mêlée at the Village Centre walkway. Nicole herself only barely avoided being knocked over by the jostling cameramen as she walked towards the Minerva Theatre.

It was good to be back in the bosom of her family. So much had happened since she had last been in Sydney and she felt comfortable returning to her home city. There was time to show Tom some of the sights and for an outing to the famous Sydney Opera House to see the Sydney Theatre Company's production of Anton Chekhov's *The Three Sisters*.

When they returned to the USA, Nicole was looking forward to starting work shortly in a new movie, a gangster film called *Billy Bathgate*, starring Dustin Hoffman, in which she had secured the only female role. But there was something else on the autumn agenda. Tom's divorce from Mimi Rogers became final in October. Now he was free to ask Nicole to marry him and he wasted little time in doing so.

It was while the lavish refurbishment of their new home was taking place that Tom is said to have asked Nicole to become his wife. The romantic story which eventually circulated in Hollywood was that he left a note on Nicole's pillow one night saying: 'My darling Nicole, I chased you and chased you until you finally caught me. Now will you marry me?' Nicole read the note when she woke up, flung her arms round Tom and said: 'I will, I will!' Until she met Tom, Nicole had thought she was far too independent ever to get married. But he was somebody she felt she really could spend the rest of her life with.

The wedding, they both knew, would require detailed and elaborate planning. Nicole was about to embark on *Billy*

Bathgate and Tom was also anxious that there should not be a media frenzy when he took Nicole as his bride. If they were to marry in America, she was adamant that members of her family should be there. Initially her mother's reaction to Nicole's wish to marry was to say: 'Hold on.' But they could see that Nicole had been completely swept off her feet, that she was deeply in love, and would not wait.

Exactly one week before Christmas 1990, Antony and Janelle Kidman and Nicole's sister Antonia flew out of Australia for what was ostensibly a Christmas break with Nicole and Tom in the United States. Since Nicole was working on *Billy Bathgate*, they had to fly to her if the Kidmans wanted to enjoy a family Christmas together. But their ultimate destination was not the couple's California home but Telluride, a scenic ski resort at the foot of the snowy Rocky Mountains in northern Colorado.

At the former mining town Tom and Nicole had rented from a Chicago businessman a fabulous $2 million house with spectacular views of the snow-capped Rockies in which to become man and wife. To ensure secrecy, the rental arrangements had been negotiated by intermediaries and the owner was under the impression his house was being rented by a Hollywood agent for a Christmas Eve party. In a further effort to keep their wedding a secret, the couple had bought their marriage licence elsewhere in Colorado.

On 24 December the stately log-house was filled with a profusion of beautiful flower arrangements, including a gorgeous willow arbour with red roses and white lilies intertwined. As the sun began to sink low over Telluride, casting a glint on the snow, Nicole stepped forward in front of a civil celebrant to become Tom's wife.

Wearing a beautiful white silk wedding gown with a long

train, she stood beside Tom, dressed in a black tuxedo, and exchanged with him marriage vows which they had written themselves. Behind her stood Antonia as her bridesmaid. Also looking on as Tom and Nicole became man and wife were Dustin Hoffman and his wife, and Australian actress Deborra-Lee Furness, a long-standing friend of Nicole's, who later revealed: 'Both Tom and Nicole, as well as their families, had tears in their eyes.'

Re-living the moment years later, Nicole reflected that it was a traditional wedding and everything she had hoped for: 'It was a lovely wedding, in Colorado, in the snow, in a cute little house we had rented. Marriage was the last thing on my mind when I came to this country. I was footloose, ambitious for my career, not at all willing to be tied down to my private life. But after being with Tom for a while, the idea just overwhelmed me. I thought: "God, he's the person I really do want to be with for the rest of my life." God knows we didn't plan it. It just happened.' She added: 'I had no doubt from the minute I got married that it was going to be my only marriage.'

There were excited claps and cheers echoing around the Telluride house when Tom was told 'You may kiss the bride', and the celebrations went on long into the night. The couple smothered each other with hugs and kisses and there were whoops of delight as midnight struck heralding the start of Christmas Day and Nicole's first day of married life as Mrs Cruise.

Importantly for the couple, they had covered their tracks so efficiently that there was not a pressman nor a photographer in sight to record the happy event. The Telluride locals, some of whom eventually latched on to the couple's secret, remained loyal and tight-lipped. But once the nuptials had become public knowledge, they said the town had not enjoyed such fame since the infamous outlaw Butch Cassidy had pulled off his first bank robbery there 100 years earlier. Tom and Nicole were so enamoured of Telluride, and it was to have such romantic memories for them, that they were eventually to buy land there and have a home of their own built.

Their wedding secret came out when Nicole telephoned her uncle Barry Fawcett back in Sydney to tell him the good news. 'You could have knocked me down with a feather,' he was reported as saying. 'I knew they were very fond of each other but we had no hint there was a wedding in the air. I'd say it was the showbusiness secret of the year.' Nicole's aunt Linda Fawcett said: 'They rang here on Christmas Day. They are very happy. She said all the normal things that brides say.' On Boxing Day Nicole called Sydney radio journalist Peter Ford to confirm her exciting news. 'She was blissfully happy,' he said. 'They are very much in love and Nicole was ecstatic when she called.'

News of the wedding took the media by surprise, and by the time TV and pressmen had descended on Telluride, Nicole and Tom were slipping quietly out of the ski resort. Nicole had been given only four days' leave of absence from the *Billy Bathgate* production and she was due back on set in North Carolina. During her filming commitments she and Tom were able to live in a rented beach house on the exclusive Figure Eight Island, where at least their privacy was guaranteed. Visitors to the island required a security pass and it was accessible only by helicopter or by boat.

Nicole and Tom agreed that they would not allow themselves to be separated for more than two weeks at a stretch. They were determined not to be driven apart by work and vowed that wherever they were in the world they would spend at least one night together every fortnight, even if it meant flying vast distances. And they remained true to that promise throughout their marriage. Nicole decided she would also remain Nicole Kidman rather than become Mrs Cruise. She had been brought up to be a woman in her own right and marrying the hottest movie star in the world – Tom had recently been voted Sexiest Man Alive – was not going to force her to change her name.

Just three weeks after their wedding they were briefly separated by work when Tom went to Los Angeles to attend the American Cinema Awards, where he was presented by Sean Connery with a Distinguished Achievement in Cinema honour. There he described marriage to Nicole, who remained in North Carolina filming, as 'absolutely wonderful' and added: 'Officially we will be on our honeymoon for the rest of our lives.'

Within weeks of tying the knot Nicole went on television to say, among other things, that Tom was the sexiest man alive. 'I love married life. I love being married,' she said. 'It's incredible – I share my life with someone that I love so much.' The TV interview included an unscheduled appearance by Tom, who said: 'I'm the happiest I have ever been. It's fantastic, absolutely incredible.'

Just twenty-three years old, Nicole probably had no inkling at that time of the much wider consequences of becoming Mrs Tom Cruise. Landing the *Days of Thunder* role and being romantically linked to Cruise raised her profile considerably, but by becoming his wife she entered an altogether different league. 'I gave up my whole life in Australia for love,' she said tellingly. 'It's such an addictive emotion.'

Now, everybody seemed to mention her name in the same breath as her husband's. Like another high-profile Hollywood husband-and-wife couple Bruce and Demi (Willis and Moore), 'Tom-and-Nicole' tripped off the tongue perhaps all too easily. But the double-first-name fame game spelled danger. Those who loved Nicole as the thoroughly decent, spirited, independent, supremely talented young woman from Sydney's north shore they knew her to be, were fearful that the delightful individuality that made her so special might be lost under the weight of being Mrs Tom Cruise.

CHAPTER 8

Going Dutch with Drew

*'When I met her, I said I had two important questions:
"Can you cross your eyes? And can you lose your
Australian accent?"'*
    – ROBERT BENTON, DIRECTOR OF *BILLY BATHGATE*

While *Days of Thunder* had been nearing completion
in Florida, Nicole was already eagerly looking
ahead to her next movie project. Her agent Sam
Cohn had sent her several scripts to peruse and Nicole knew
just the kind of role she was looking for. She had just seen *The
Fabulous Baker Boys*, a smoothly made and hugely entertaining
romantic comedy-drama about two piano-playing brothers
who find an attractive young singer to give some much needed
glamorous pep to their dying act. Michelle Pfeiffer, as the
sexy-surly singer Susie Diamond, had made the most of the
role, and of her femininity, sandwiched between two real-life
acting brothers, Beau and Jeff Bridges. If only there were a film

role like that for Nicole Kidman, Nicole wished fervently.

Not long afterwards she believed she might have found one when Cohn delivered to her a script for a new Walt Disney movie, *Billy Bathgate*. Also enclosed was the novel by E. L. Doctorow on which the script had been based. As always when script and book arrived together, Nicole opted to read the book first and she was captivated at once by the character of Drew Preston, the silky 1930s mobster's moll she was being sounded out to play. It looked a strong, challenging role and she counted herself lucky as most actresses her age were being offered parts in teenage romance, or college campus stories.

Set in the world of New York gangsters in the mid 1930s, the book tells the story of a young boy from the Bronx who works his way up to become a protégé of Dutch Schultz, once a notorious real-life king of the underworld. Stepping elegantly into this violent world comes 22-year-old Drew Preston, a mysterious, ravishing, high-spirited socialite, married to an older man, who gets her kicks from mixing and sleeping with gangsters. But the freedom with which she dispenses her favours among such dangerous men ultimately lands her in grave peril.

Nicole saw at once that it was a good story which could make a great film and that Drew Preston was a strong character she could happily get her teeth into on screen. E. L. Doctorow's books with their intricate plots and verbose writing had always proved a big challenge to film-makers. His first, *Welcome to Hard Times*, became a gripping western, starring Henry Fonda, and Milos Forman had made a good job of *Ragtime*.

Nicole saw Drew Preston as someone who enjoyed taking risks, leaned towards the wild side and tended to get bored easily. As one who delighted in the adrenaline rush of daredevil sports, was willing to take risks in life, and resorted to making lists when bored, Nicole believed she understood quite a bit about Drew. When Cohn subsequently telephoned to tell Nicole that Dustin Hoffman was going to play the male lead and there was genuine interest in her playing the female lead, she could scarcely believe her ears. Cohn had already paved the way by sending the *Billy Bathgate* production team a show-reel tape of her work.

Robert Benton, who was set to direct *Billy Bathgate*, had heard all the talk about Nicole in *Dead Calm* and decided to see the movie for himself. It confirmed in his own mind the good reports of her and he invited Nicole to have dinner with him to discuss the project. Nicole felt that they really clicked when they met, but with a $40 million movie Benton had to be realistic. He was extremely concerned whether her vowels were too Australian for her to be able to turn herself convincingly into a New York aristocrat. He required her to be Park Avenue not north shore Sydney and he needed to be sure there would not be a trace of Aussie accent in any word that Drew Preston uttered if he was to entrust the role to Nicole. He wondered whether she would be up to it. Benton recalls: 'When I met her, I said I had two important questions: "Can you cross your eyes? And can you lose your Australian accent?" '

Nicole was more than prepared to try. Benton gave her the name of a voice coach, with whom she worked day and night for two weeks on perfecting a New York accent. Summoned back to New York after a fortnight for a progress meeting with Benton, she left the director in no doubt that she would not let him down. 'I had serious doubts that Nicole could entirely drop the Aussie accent in such a short time,' he said. 'We met again in New York and, when she walked into the meeting, she spoke in a perfect upper-class eastern American school accent,' he recalls. 'And she crossed her eyes.'

By the time Nicole went for a further audition, this time with Dustin Hoffman at the actor's home, she had read the *Billy Bathgate* novel three times and had prepared herself thoroughly. She badly wanted the role, not least because it was the only part for a woman in the film, and was made all the more eye-catching by contrasting sharply with male characters who were bristling with macho power, real or imagined.

Benton accompanied her to meet Dustin and said encouragingly: 'Well, babe, I don't hear any Sydney in your voice.' Nicole could be forgiven for being scared at meeting Dustin for the first time. Dustin Hoffman had first shot to stardom the year Nicole was born. In 1967 in *The Graduate*, he had become the most talked-about actor of the year for his acclaimed portrayal of a young man just out of college, wondering what life was all about, who finds himself seduced by an older woman played by Anne Bancroft. Since then Hoffman had built up an impressive body of work in a variety of roles in movies such as *Midnight Cowboy, Little Big Man, Papillon, Lenny, All the President's Men* and *Kramer vs. Kramer*, which had been directed by Robert Benton and for which Dustin won an Oscar. Nicole was not wrong in her assessment of him as one of the best actors of his generation.

Nicole's nerves were not helped by her awareness that her height might once again be against her. Dustin was several inches smaller than her and she felt uneasy as they sat down and he quietly began observing her.

After the initial introductions, Hoffman's first question to Nicole was: 'Have you read the book?' When she said she had, the actor told her that it was the first affirmative reply he had been given by any of the other actresses up for the role. This counted in her favour and came as a welcome, but huge, surprise to Nicole. She was frankly astonished that anyone who wanted the role of Drew Preston could be so uncommitted as not even to bother to read the novel. Nicole had always been told how motivated and determined American actresses were so she was even further amazed to hear that two of her *Billy Bathgate* competitors had not even troubled to read the script.

Heartened by the fact that Nicole had read the book not just once but three times, Hoffman suggested they try a scene together. This was where her preparation paid off handsomely and she was brimming with confidence. This allowed her to play around with Drew Preston for Dustin Hoffman's approval in no fewer than eight different ways – moving elegantly around the room, pausing to touch something, lighting up a cigarette, improvising. 'Basically I had fun,' she said.

When she had finished, Dustin Hoffman did not say a word. Disconsolately Nicole headed for home believing she had blown her chances. But no sooner had she left than Dustin was on the phone to Tom Cruise. First he called the office saying he needed to talk to Tom urgently, then he phoned his home and then his car phone. Finally he got hold of Tom in an editing room and told him he wanted Nicole in the movie. Tom started leaping up and down and hugging everyone in the room. 'Where did you find her?' asked Dustin, who was always telling Tom how lucky he was in life. 'Not only is this woman beautiful and she's apparently, for some unknown reason, in love with you, but she's incredibly talented too.' Next day Nicole's agent Sam Cohn telephoned her to confirm that the part was hers. Hoffman had made up his mind almost immediately.

Nicole played Drew as a high-spirited, sexy and desirable woman capable of casting a spell over even the most dangerous of men – and who knows it and enjoys it. 'I'm not his girl. He's my gangster,' she says at one point, displaying her taste for danger. Always elegantly dressed and stylishly glamorous, she shone like a beacon among the bloody carnage and brutal slaughter that punctuates the story and she was the perfect feminine foil for Dustin Hoffman's maniacal moments of explosive violence.

Set in 1938 after the end of Prohibition and after Al Capone had ended up in prison for tax evasion, Robert Benton's film opens with an important scene for Nicole as Dutch takes revenge on a once-trusted lieutenant, Bo Weinberg, played by Bruce Willis. Bo is being ferried up New York's East River with his feet encased in cement, a watery grave destined to be his chillingly final reward for betraying his boss. Also on board, silently witnessing Bo's horrific demise, is Bo's lover, Mrs Drew Preston, an elegant and stylish young socialite, and Loren Dean as Billy Bathgate. He is a young lad from the Bronx with a bleak future, who is dazzled by the aura of power surrounding gangsters and gets himself hired by Dutch as his protégé.

With Bo at the bottom of the river, Drew soon transfers her affections to Dutch, who instructs Billy to be her minder. But Dutch's days as untouchable king of the underworld are numbered. The Feds are closing in on him and he is also up in court for tax evasion. His cohorts eventually contrive to have the case heard in upstate New York where a favourable verdict is anticipated, and there Dutch is joined by Drew and Billy, with the former posing as his 'governess' to avoid further mud being publicly slung at Dutch. But Billy and Drew are drawing closer together and become lovers at just about the time Dutch realises Drew is a witness to Bo's death and that she could testify against him. When Dutch sends his gunmen to bump her off, Billy has to come to her rescue.

Anxious to learn all she could while putting in her best performance, Nicole was quietly in awe of Dustin Hoffman as filming progressed. 'He was always thinking, always observant, spontaneous and quick, and came up with idea after idea.' Happily for everyone, Nicole found that her height was not an issue. 'I am four inches taller than Dustin, and he loved it. Dustin played a cold-blooded killer who towered over every-body, at least in his own mind, including his five foot eleven girlfriend, yours truly.'

Nicole was not averse to a little teasing of her illustrious co-star. Cruise, who frequently visited the set to give Nicole his support and regularly sent her flowers when he was absent, remembers that at one point in the filming Nicole startled Dustin in the middle of a very serious scene by jokingly barking at him like a dog. Nicole was pleasantly surprised to find that Dustin, for all his immense talent as an actor, was not averse to displaying a sense of fun when making a movie. He also encouraged her to voice her opinions about the way their scenes together should be shot.

Benton, too, placed tremendous trust in her. Nicole had grown in confidence since *Days of Thunder* where she had been understandably tense. Now the director was prepared to give her a great deal of freedom. He felt Nicole understood Drew Preston far better than he ever could so he told her to deliver Drew as she saw fit. So faultless was Nicole's American accent that the film crew were baffled when, after a long day's filming had come to an end, Nicole would revert to her natural Aussie intonations. 'Is this some kind of joke?' a perplexed lighting man politely asked of Benton.

The emerging affair between Drew and Billy was largely filmed in Saratoga Springs, about 300 kilometres upstate north of New York City, and the production took extraordinary security measures when Nicole came to film a full-frontal yet tasteful nude scene in which Drew emerges from a skinny-dip in a lake watched by an admiring Billy. All access roads leading to the Lake Corinth location were sealed off and guards combed the nearby woods searching for any persistent paparazzi. Bravely Nicole took to the water on a day when there was a biting autumn wind and the temperature at Saratoga Springs was a goosebump-inducing 15 degrees.

After three weeks filming in Saratoga Springs during which Tom Cruise was for some of the time a supportive visitor to the set, production moved to the streets of New York where Manhattan Avenue was cast back to the thirties with the appearance of dozens of vintage cars and many hundreds of extras dressed in the fashions of the thirties. Then, for Nicole, it was off to Charlotte and Hamlet, North Carolina, which brought back happy memories for the actress. She had been in Charlotte almost a year previously filming *Days of Thunder* with Tom. But, for Dustin Hoffman, the Hamlet location brought great sadness with news of the death of his father.

By all accounts *Billy Bathgate* was not the smoothest of productions and Nicole had to be recalled from Ireland, where she was by then filming her next movie, *Far and Away* with Tom Cruise, to re-shoot scenes including the ending just weeks before the movie opened. It had been hit by a sudden change in release date from March 1992 to November 1991 which made for some hurried re-scheduling.

Robert Benton, however, was exhilarated by Nicole's performance. 'She was phenomenal,' he said. 'Her American accent was perfect. Her role was very difficult and challenging but her performance was utterly flawless. She was always so prepared. There isn't a single moment I would change. I'm betting this movie will establish Nicole as one of the major American movie stars. Her talent is huge.'

Dustin Hoffman, who gave the Cruises a set of bowling balls to show his appreciation, agreed. 'Nicole stretched even beyond her incredible work in *Dead Calm*,' he said. 'Nicole's talent just leaps out at you. She's entirely convincing and natural up on that screen. Her instincts are unerring.'

Although the film itself garnered mixed notices, Nicole – who, importantly, had second billing – won rave reviews when *Billy Bathgate* opened in New York in November 1991. The *Wall Street Journal* said the movie 'only comes to life when Kidman takes centre stage'. It added: 'Ms Kidman, the Australian actress best known here as Tom Cruise's wife, is just wonderful as Drew Preston. She gets across the boredom that makes Drew ready for anything. When Drew is the focus, the story takes on the mischief that is missing everywhere else.'

The *Village Voice* said Kidman 'has a compelling intensity. She is wanton and innocent in a way that nothing else in the movie ever manages.' The *New York Post* wondered how Nicole had managed to lose her Australian accent so convincingly. 'She is as disarming as she is meant to be, especially when she drops her drawers in front of Billy's feverish adolescent gaze,' it noted, referring to Nicole's tasteful nude scene. The *New York Times* called Nicole 'a beauty with a sense of humour'. But the reviewer felt she had been cut short before she could really sizzle on the screen as 'someone who immediately registers as an original'.

The highly favourable reviews were a shot in the arm for Nicole from every perspective. Not only did they earn her a Golden Globe nomination from Hollywood's foreign press, but they also went a long way to silencing the gossips who liked to think that she had only won the role of Drew Preston on the strength of her relationship with Tom Cruise and his friendship with Dustin Hoffman.

CHAPTER 9

Luck of the Irish

'We like being together twenty-four hours a day'
– TOM CRUISE

Many Americans believed Nicole Kidman had come over from Australia, married Tom Cruise and then become an actress. This commonly held public misconception proved extremely frustrating for her and Nicole found herself all too frequently explaining to the ignorant that she had in fact been working as an actress for fully ten years.

Always a firm believer in the strength of intention – of setting herself goals and then following her decisions through without deflection – she now had a career plan secretly mapped out for herself for the next five years, which was to make a least five films and to appear on the New York stage. She had no intention to allow her own identity as an actress to get swallowed up in the swirl of publicity which, Nicole had rapidly discovered, accompanied her charismatic husband Tom Cruise's every move.

For someone keen to carve her own niche, it was therefore surprising that she agreed to team up with Tom again for her next film, *Far and Away*. Much as she loved Tom and the break he had given her into Hollywood, the last thing she wanted was to be perceived as an actress out to build a career by riding on her famous husband's coat tails, but by pairing up with him on screen once more so soon after *Days of Thunder*, she was in danger of undermining the impact of her good work in *Billy Bathgate*.

To be fair, she could point to the fact that *Far and Away*, a sweeping historical epic, did offer her a strong female leading role opposite her husband. She was very much in love with him and he with her, and much of *Far and Away* would be filmed in Ireland. They wanted to be together as much as possible as Tom was anxious to avoid the lengthy separations which had caused problems in his first marriage. The big-budget film, to be directed by former *Happy Days* television star Ron Howard, whose credits as director included *Backdraft*, *Cocoon* and *Parenthood*, offered them months of togetherness on what they both believed to be a worthwhile project.

Whenever one or other of the couple was asked about their other half, they rarely missed an opportunity to express how deeply they felt about each other. In a TV interview with Oprah Winfrey just before filming started on *Far and Away*, Tom and Nicole giggled away and snuggled up to each other like lovestruck teenagers. 'We like being together twenty-four hours a day,' said Tom when Oprah asked them if they did everything together. (By the end of filming *Far and Away*, however, they were so anxious not to be seen as a double act on screen that they insisted on conducting promotional interviews separately. They were also quick to counter any suggestion that Tom had used his influence to have Nicole cast as his leading lady. Tom contended it was preposterous to think he could tell a director of Ron Howard's standing how to cast his film.)

Far and Away was in essence a tale of nineteenth-century immigrants making their way in the New World, with Tom and Nicole playing class-crossed Irish lovers leaving western Ireland in 1892 to seek a new life together in America.

Tom played Joseph Donnelly, third son of a poor but honest Irish tenant farmer, who seeks revenge after his family home is set ablaze by the landlord's overseer. Armed with an old musket, he leaves the muddy streets of his village on a donkey and heads off to kill the landlord, Christie. But he is discovered hiding in the stables by the landlord's daughter, Shannon, played by Nicole, who stabs him in the leg with a pitchfork. As he staggers wounded out of the stables, Joseph takes a shot at Christie but the musket is old and faulty and he winds up injured and locked in a bedroom upstairs while the authorities are summoned.

Soon Joseph and the pampered but spirited Shannon realise they have one vital thing in common. They are both desperate to escape the, albeit very different, lives they have in Ireland. Joseph is fed up with oppression and poverty, Shannon is straining to be rid of the tightest of leashes held by mother. Seeking pastures new, they become unlikely travelling companions and head off by ship for America. But within minutes of reaching Boston, Shannon loses the fortune she has brought with her. Now penniless, Joseph introduces her to his own kind

— hard-drinking Irish immigrants who enjoy watching bare-knuckle fights. To her chagrin, Shannon has to pose as Joseph's sister and share a room with him in a brothel, as well as taking a job plucking chickens to earn a crust. Joseph, meanwhile, discovers that his own boxing skills can elevate him to a new kind of American aristocracy almost overnight and he battles it out nightly with his bare fists, going more than thirty rounds at a time. His and Shannon's aim is to save up for a horse and wagon to make the trek to Oklahoma for the Cherokee Strip Land Race. But, having struggled against their true feelings for each other for so long, their growing affection becomes their downfall.

In view of Tom and Nicole's recent off-screen passionate affair and subsequent marriage, one particular scene in *Far and Away* prompted the special interest of cinema audiences. It occurred when Tom, as Joseph, is locked up in a bedroom after his vain attempt to kill his oppressive landlord. Wounded in the leg by Shannon's pitchfork thrust, Joseph lies with eyes closed in a semi-coma on a bed, naked but for a strategically placed pudding bowl protecting his modesty. Enter Nicole as the lively Shannon whose curiosity gets the better of her. Tiptoe-ing up to the bed, she gingerly lifts the lid of the bowl to take a quick peek underneath before turning away to register a smirking expression of wonder and approval. For Tom's millions of female fans, Nicole's awed gaze told them everything they had ever fantasised about their idol.

Naturally there was much merriment on set when it came to filming such an intimate scene between husband and wife. Director Howard felt the scene was fully justified because it let audiences in on Shannon's mischievous nature. But of course there was the added spice of their being a real life couple.

During rehearsals Tom kept joking: 'I need a bigger bowl!' and wore something under the pudding bowl. But when it came to the actual take, he was, unbeknown to Nicole, stark naked. Her look of genuine surprise as she lifted the bowl and peeped under it was exactly what director Ron Howard was looking for.

After filming in Montana, Tom and Nicole moved with the production to Ireland. They both had Irish ancestors and they were keen to explore the Emerald Isle. They fell in love with Dublin and marvelled at the beauty of the countryside and coastline when they moved into a rented cottage on the west coast in Dingle, County Kerry. When time allowed they went for leisurely walks and felt as if they were on honeymoon again. It was noticeable on set how openly affectionate they were to each other, kissing and cuddling and laughing together.

But it was not all plain sailing. Nicole had to film several scenes on horseback, dressed in a corset and three layers of wool petticoats, bloomers, stockings and boots. In the height of summer it made for an uncomfortable ride. As her confidence grew on horseback, she was not averse to challenging Tom to the odd race. She whooped with delight on the occasions her mount managed to pass his.

Tom's fight scenes were carefully choreographed but he was unhappy with some of the moments when it looked as though the punches from stuntmen had missed their target. Ron Howard stepped in and reminded them they were there to brawl. 'But none of them wanted to be the man who broke Tom Cruise's nose,' Tom later recalled. 'Finally I said: "Look, hit me and let's get this over so we can move on."' Nicole was the one who was heavily garbed for most of the film while Tom was the one who stripped to the waist and showed off his physique.

She liked seeing her husband naked to the waist as the champion bare-fisted fighter and at one point teasingly shouted out: 'Nice chest!' But she could hardly bear it when a blow from a stuntman connected with her husband's handsome face. She hated to see him getting hurt.

In May 1992 *Far and Away* was screened at the Cannes Film Festival prior to an almost simultaneous release in countries around the world which required Nicole and Tom to embark on a gruelling round of promotional interviews. The movie was not given an overly enthusiastic reception in Cannes where, bizarrely, the couple had to deny a rumour that they were about to play the Duke and Duchess of York, Prince Andrew and Sarah Ferguson. Once the rumour had started, the mere fact that Nicole had red hair like 'Fergie' seemed to convince the less responsible members of the press that the rumour was fact. It was not.

In all his many promotional interviews over the ensuing few weeks – he did no fewer than 150 in two days – Tom Cruise was noticeably always highly supportive of Nicole. 'I just think she is going to be one of the greats, unquestionably,' he told one interviewer. 'I saw her in *Dead Calm* and I remember thinking: This woman is enormously talented, has an incredible presence, is very poised and very bright and her choices as an actress are extraordinary. She's just exceptional. It doesn't take a genius to figure out that she's amazingly talented – the real thing. Being able to act with her was very romantic.'

In America the critics had a field day with *Far and Away*, one even dubbing it 'Flat and Awry'. The *Washington Post* described it as 'an epic Irish Spring commercial', and a 'doddering, bloated bit of corn', and added that Cruise 'has never seemed so lightweight'. But there was praise for Nicole. The *New York Post* commented on Cruise: 'He's a movie star, it's true, but it's Nicole Kidman who seems to be the genuine article.' The *Post's* critic added that Kidman 'at least brings some ferocity to her performance . . . her forcefulness makes her co-star's work appear all the more paltry'. The *New York Daily News* reported: 'Kidman is wonderfully frisky and utterly charming as the rebellious upper-class Irish lass. Cruise is more subdued . . .' The *New York Times* declared: 'Miss Kidman is wonderfully feisty and comic.' And over on the west coast, the much respected *Los Angeles Times* was unimpressed: 'Always preposterous and occasionally tedious, the bulk of *Far and Away* underlines the pitfalls of making a great-looking movie with not a whiff of originality to its name.' Luckily, one thing Tom Cruise had taught Nicole was never to read reviews.

In London the movie was mauled by the British press hours before Princess Diana attended its charity premiere. Derek Malcolm in the *Guardian* wrote: '*Far and Away* strains the credulity so fast and so far that there's almost nothing left of it within five minutes. The film lasts 140 minutes which is a long time to hide under the seat for fear of seriously damaging your brain cells.' Malcolm wondered why so much money had been spent on 'much mush'. The *Daily Telegraph* said the film's strength was mainly visual but the storyline was 'the stuff of costumed soap, heavily perfumed with peat'.

Despite what the critics said, the film was handsomely mounted and amiably performed, even if it lacked dramatic urgency – Joseph and Shannon take almost the entire picture to get together. Visually it was stunning and it was notable for being the first narrative, non effects-oriented Hollywood feature film in more than two decades to have been shot on

65mm stock and released in 70mm which gave it a widescope appearance on cinema screens.

At least there was a warmer welcome for Nicole, as was to be expected, when she and Tom went to Australia for the film's opening down under. The screening was followed a couple of weeks later by Nicole's twenty-fifth birthday and she was thrown a surprise party at a Potts Point, Sydney restaurant where around seventy guests quaffed Louis Roederer Crystal Rose champagne and grazed on Atlantic salmon and fillet of veal. Then she and Tom headed up to the Blue Mountains for a romantic weekend.

On Wednesday 3 June, about 6,000 fans thronged Greater Union Cinema in George Street, Sydney, for the *Far and Away* premiere. They had come to see the local girl from Longueville putting on the style with her Hollywood-hero husband. Nicole did not disappoint, looking stunning in a black, pin-striped suit with the mini-skirt trimmed in black lace, and adorned only by a filigree gold necklace scattered with diamonds. She looked every inch a star. At the party afterwards at Kitty O'Shea's, an Irish pub situated close to Sydney's best family-run hotel, Sullivans, in Oxford Street, Paddington, the Guinness and Irish whiskey ran freely as Nicole and Tom toasted the film's success with 300 guests.

The couple's huge international promotional push paid off at the box office. But at almost every interview Nicole did to promote the film, there was one recurring question: 'Are you pregnant?' When she said she was not, the follow-up question was invariably, 'Do you and Tom want a family?' Yes, she said, they did, even telling one inquisitor she wanted 'at least three children'. She was also often asked about what it was like to live in Tom's giant shadow. 'I wish I could be seen as me. But then I fell in love with somebody and I'm not going to kick myself for that, because that's one of the things you want to do in life. And he makes me so happy,' she said. One thing she was always keen to stress was that her relationship with Tom had begun on *Days of Thunder* only after he had broken up with his first wife Mimi. 'He was obviously married so we were ethical in that regard,' she said. 'But certainly after the film ended we knew we wanted to spend the rest of our lives together.'

One month after Nicole celebrated her twenty-fifth birthday in 1992, Tom Cruise reached the age of thirty. Ever since he and Nicole had married, the couple had regularly talked about having a family, and a baby was all that was missing from their lives. To the watching world they appeared to have everything else – a solid, loving marriage, luxurious homes, immense wealth, an exciting and glamorous lifestyle, and the adoration of millions. They took adventurous holidays in exotic locations and their behaviour when they were not working, either together or on separate movies, suggested they were enjoying a never-ending honeymoon. Tom openly admitted Nicole had made him happier than he had ever been at any time in his life.

But the milestone age of thirty prompted Tom with Nicole's enthusiastic consent to explore the possibilities of adopting a baby. They both wanted a family but, in the eighteen months they had been married, a baby had not been forthcoming. For Tom it was not the first time he had had to face up to the fact that he had not been able to become a father.

Now he and Nicole decided they were ready to give a home to an underprivileged child and, in early December 1992, adoption papers were filed in Palm Beach, Florida. But unfortunately for Nicole and Tom, their plans leaked out to the press.

Furious at the breach of confidence and with great regret, the couple decided to withdraw their adoption plans. This was not a fit of pique but was prompted by the very real fear that the leaked news could endanger the chances of the identity of the child's natural mother remaining secret.

In early January, however, Tom Cruise and Nicole became the proud parents of an adopted nine-pound baby girl they named Isabella Jane Kidman Cruise. The baby was born to a poor family in a Florida hospital and the adoption was finalised on 15 January. Nicole arrived from Los Angeles and Tom flew in from Memphis, where he was making a new movie called *The Firm*, to collect the infant from the hospital in Miami. As she held Isabella for the first time, Nicole was misty-eyed. She herself had enjoyed such a happy family childhood and she swore she would do her level best to give Isabella the same. She also intended to make Isabella's life as normal as she possibly could given that her adoptive parents were two famous movie stars. The delighted couple took Isabella straight to their home in Los Angeles where they had prepared a nursery for her and there they remained for several days bonding with the baby.

Nicole's life, of course, was never going to be the same again, but she was confident that she could handle mother-hood and also continue with her acting career. 'She took to being a mum so easily,' says a close Hollywood associate. 'She adored Isabella right from the moment she set eyes on her. She looked thoroughly comfortable and at ease with a baby in her arms.'

Two years later, Nicole and Tom were enjoying parenthood so much that they adopted a second child, a baby son they called Connor.

CHAPTER 10

A Role to Die For

'When you're that beautiful and married to a superstar your talent can seem secondary'
— DIRECTOR JOEL SCHUMACHER

I t is the grouse of most actresses that there are never enough decent, strong roles for women, and for Nicole Kidman there was a growing frustration with the cinema industry as she settled into the responsibilities of motherhood. After her experiences on *Far and Away* she realised there was much to be said for avoiding the burden of having to carry a major Hollywood movie with a massive multi-million-dollar budget. She felt confined in such films, but the alternative did not appear promising because the kind of roles she had once enjoyed in Australia in *Vietnam*, and *Bangkok Hilton* on TV, and in the movie *Dead Calm*, were few and far between and hard to come by.

Hollywood's method of working was to build a major movie around a big star they knew could carry such a film, a bankable star who would virtually guarantee a commercial success. Nicole was not yet in that league. She was still on the B list of Hollywood actresses. Nevertheless, her instruction to her agent was to bother not about the size of the cheque but about the quality of the role on offer.

Nicole had come into acting with high ideals and had tried not to lose sight of them even when she was sucked into the Hollywood jungle, but the truth of the matter was that she was finding it more difficult to step out from under Tom Cruise's shadow than she could possibly have imagined. 'When you're that beautiful and married to a superstar your talent can seem secondary,' was the astute observation of film director Joel Schumacher, who was later to cast her in *Batman Forever*. 'But she is a really strong, really inspired young actress.'

Unfortunately for Nicole, not everyone in Hollywood had Schumacher's perception. As she searched for that elusive female role which would really show what she was capable of and would do her talent justice, however, Nicole knew she could hardly complain about life. She was enjoying being married to Tom and, now she was revelling in life as a mother too, she came to realise that she did not have to suffer for her art as she had once thought. She could look at stars such as Meryl Streep and Dustin Hoffman and their respective families and see that they had great lives and they were not exactly suffering. So why shouldn't she enjoy herself?

Nicole's father had always encouraged his daughters to think there was nothing they could not do physically if they put their minds to it and Nicole made adventurous use of her leisure time playing golf, tennis, going horse-riding and joining Tom in his more dangerous pursuits such as aerobatics, dive-bombing the ocean and diving with reef sharks in the Bahamas. Occasionally, though, this naturally inquisitive trait to have a go at anything physically challenging landed Nicole in trouble.

In 1996 on holiday in Italy with Tom she was eager to go hiking at Stromboli, an active volcano on an island off the Italian coast, and set off wearing beige chinos and black sneakers with a guide as her only companion. She sprained her ankle and was missing for eight and a half hours. Tom, who had stayed behind, became concerned for his wife's safety when there was no sign of her as darkness fell. He was starting to panic and fear the worst when he still had not seen or heard from Nicole by the early hours of the morning.

Eventually a distraught Nicole was rescued by two Italian skydivers who escorted her to a yacht where they helped her to radio Tom who was by now frantic with worry. 'It was like one of those things out of a bad movie,' she says. 'I was sobbing Thomas, Thomas.'

By the time Tom arrived, Nicole was clearly suffering from the shock of her ordeal and was finding it difficult to string words together that made much sense. She kept saying 'Thomas these are very nice people. If they offer you coffee, you must accept.' Tom stared at his wife in bewilderment but, anxious not to aggravate Nicole's fragile and distressed state of mind, he took up the Italian boat owner's offer of a cup of coffee. He swigged it back as quickly as he could, thanked her rescuers profusely, and led Nicole gently away.

That same year, 1996, Nicole was unfortunate to dislocate a shoulder while skiing in Colorado. Another skier, a six foot four-tall, powerfully built man, came whizzing down the slope screaming at Nicole to get out of the way. But it was too late and he crashed violently and painfully into her.

On another occasion, after a photo shoot at a farmhouse in Charleston, Nicole had a deeply alarming ride in a helicopter. The weather was worsening by the minute as the pilot took off and after narrowly missing a set of power lines, he made an emergency landing deep in the countryside. Eventually, a startled farmer opened his front door to find a top movie star politely asking if she could come in and use his telephone to summon further transport to take her on her journey.

Once she and Tom had adopted Isabella and Connor, Nicole decided to temper her dangerous pursuits somewhat.

Over the next few years Nicole continued working steadily but the films she made followed a pattern of middling commercial success and modest critical praise. She made *Malice* with Alec Baldwin, a convoluted, twisting thriller directed by Harold Becker, and *My Life*, a poignant drama with Michael Keaton, in which she played a young wife who is expecting her first baby but then finds her husband has terminal cancer.

With the help of slinky black dresses, perfect hair, perfect red lips and a husky voice, Nicole also turned in a smart, sexy, deliberately over-the-top turn as Dr Chase Meridian, a criminal psychologist who sets her romantic sights on Gotham's hero Batman, played by Val Kilmer, in the second Batman sequel, *Batman Forever*. Long-time admirer director Joel Schumacher admitted he had been keeping an eye on Nicole since *Dead Calm*. 'You meet a lot of beautiful people in this business,' he said, 'but there's something almost luminous about her. I wish I had a clause in my contract that said Nicole Kidman had to be in every one of my movies.'

For so gifted an actress as Nicole, these were movies that kept her in the public eye without revealing or exploiting the depth of performance she was so patently willing and able to produce given the right material. They were roles which patently failed to stretch her talent. And she was becoming more and more concerned about it.

Indeed, there came a point when Nicole had not worked for a year and was becoming desperately frustrated at her lack of suitable opportunities. Tom, meanwhile, was working all the time on a string of movies and, although she was pleased for him rather than being jealous of his success, it all prompted her to stop and re-evaluate her career.

Nicole actually considered moving back to Australia but that was impractical from the point of view of her marriage. Instead, she went back to school at New York's famous Actors Studio and pondered her next move – which turned out to be a masterstroke.

Nicole got to hear about a new movie being made by Gus Van Sant featuring a chillingly ambitious TV weather girl called Suzanne Stone. Suzanne is obsessed with becoming famous and she is so fiercely determined to make it big in TV that she seduces her teenage lover into killing the husband who stands in the way of her advancement.

Meg Ryan was reputed to be just one of many top-line Hollywood actresses vying for the role in the film entitled *To Die For*. But Nicole had a gut feeling that this was a project right up her street, especially in the hands of a director like Van Sant. He had stirred up no little controversy with a movie called *Drugstore Cowboy* which dared to address the fact that people take drugs because they *enjoy* them. No previous drug-themed film had displayed the honesty or originality of Van Sant's movie about a self-confessed and totally unrepentant drug addict, played by Matt Dillon. Van Sant had followed up with *My Own Private Idaho*, a title taken from a B-F52s song, about two very different young street hustlers, starring River Phoenix and Keanu Reeves.

Nicole just knew *To Die For* could be a really special movie. The problem was that Van Sant was unfamiliar with her work. Summoning up all her courage, she picked up the telephone and called the director at his home to make an impassioned plea for the part to be hers. In a long conversation she told Van Sant she felt she really knew and completely understood this character and insisted that Suzanne Stone was one role she was destined to play. For fully an hour the director listened intently to Nicole stating her case in the emotionally charged, forcefully determined, unswerving manner that Suzanne herself might have employed. And then he gave her the part over the phone.

Nicole was thrilled. 'I read the script and loved it,' she said, 'but everyone around me said I mustn't take it. They said the character wasn't likeable and that everyone would think I was really like her. But I insisted. If I could have the chance to work in a film like that, I didn't care.' That was just as well since it was a film to be made on a budget of $11 million, minuscule by Hollywood standards, and Nicole's fee would be proportionately modest. Even that lowly budget was a struggle for Van Sant to raise and in the end he was forced to shoot *To Die For* in Canada to save money.

To Die For was loosely based on the story of Pamela Smart, a high-school teacher who in 1991 coaxed a teenager to murder her husband. Van Sant set his story in the small town of Little

Hope, New Hampshire, where sexy blonde Suzanne inveigles her way into a job as the weather girl on the town's local cable TV station. She marries Larry, played by Matt Dillon, a nice enough man from a family who run a local Italian restaurant. But as Suzanne's thirst for fame becomes an obsession, his homeliness jars with her fiercely held belief that 'You are nobody unless you are on television.' Larry is holding Suzanne back and she does not want his babies, she says, 'because a woman in my field with a baby has two strikes against her. She can't cover a royal wedding, or a revolution in South America, and pregnancy gives her blubber, and boobs out to here. It's gross.' Nothing is too gross for Suzanne when it comes to plotting to get ahead, not even fellating the right TV executive if it might mean gaining promotion.

Suzanne's warped ambition is driven by her opinion that she has to be on TV because, she muses, otherwise what is the point of doing anything worthwhile if nobody is watching? Soon she is dazzling three youngsters from her local school with her own sexy brand of local TV personality glamour. She persuades them to help her murder Larry, then lets them down with cheery brutality.

Nicole prepared for her portrayal of Suzanne Stone by closeting herself away in a hotel room in Santa Barbara for three days to soak up as many trashy TV talk shows as she could. She also made a detailed study of American women over a period of three months and spoke with nothing but an American accent during that period. As part of Suzanne's learning curve, the weather girl makes her own little TV programme. Nicole did likewise and learned how to edit it.

She was nothing short of brilliant as Suzanne Stone. Wickedly funny in the film, she won some of the best notices of her career. She played Suzanne not as some deranged bitch but as a young woman whose ambition is mis-channelled in the wrong direction. Nicole is in turn sexy, scheming, charming, murderous, vicious, coquettish, stunning, funny, dark, sharp – all in all, the most dangerous of callous femmes fatales. 'Kidman crafts a role of breathtakingly controlled artifice, dead-on timing and dizzyingly precise humour,' raved one critic.

Not only did the movie bring to an end a streak of mostly tame roles, but it also forced critics to regard Nicole not just as Mrs Tom Cruise. The film was a critical and commercial success and Nicole believed it had put her back on track as an actress. She felt she had reverted to the Australian-style movies that suited her best, movies where the emphasis was on the characters rather than the size of the budget and the special effects. It reinforced her view that the best character roles were to be found in projects by independent film-makers.

To her immense satisfaction, Nicole deservedly won the Golden Globe Best Actress award for *To Die For*. An Oscar nomination was not forthcoming, however, but her disappointment was shortlived. She had suspected she had missed out because of the number of Motion Picture Academy members who had walked out of the screenings. Nicole was in the final throes of post-production work on her next movie, *The Portrait of a Lady*, on the day she heard she had been overlooked. But she was heartened by a sympathetic fax message she received from Stanley Kubrick who said: 'You're a character actress, Nicole, they don't recognise that kind of talent.' Nicole kept the fax. 'Much better than an Academy award,' she decided.

CHAPTER 11

You're My Isabel

'Protect your talent'

– JANE CAMPION

Protect your talent. That was the watchful advice film-maker Jane Campion had thoughtfully urged upon the precocious Nicole Kidman back in 1981 when she had first spotted the gangling fourteen-year-old schoolgirl's remarkable potential as an actress and noted the youthful burning commitment which went with it.

Back then, as we have already seen, New Zealander Campion had tried to enlist Nicole for *A Girl's Own Story*, her graduation film for the Australian Film, Television, and Radio school, only to be thwarted by Nicole's headmistress who reasoned that exams were a much higher priority than a film role that would entail Nicole taking time off from her lessons.

There had been huge disappointment on both sides but Jane, some thirteen years older than the teenage Nicole, left her with a promise that they would work together at some time in the future. She even went so far as to declare that she hoped to direct Nicole in a classic one day – a remarkable thing to say to one so young. Clearly she saw in Nicole a rare talent.

As the years went by, each observed with interest as the other's career blossomed in very different ways. While Nicole had gone on to make a transition to glamorous Hollywood star and wife, Campion had won herself immense respect as a dedicated maker of movies noted for strong and interesting female characters. Her unusual examinations of female 'outsiders' had made her one of cinema's most interesting new voices. After first earning acclaim for her short films, Campion wrote and directed her first feature movie, *Sweetie*, in 1989, a darkly humorous account of an eccentric woman and her relationship with her family. Her fourth feature film, *The Piano*, a visually sumptuous tale of adultery set during the early colonization of New Zealand in the 1850s, brought her to wider international attention in 1993. *The Piano* earned Holly Hunter the Best Actress Oscar as the heroine of the piece, a woman who can hear but cannot speak and is physically unable to articulate her feelings other than through sign language and her beloved piano. Campion's chronicling of a most unusual love triangle won the film an Oscar for Best Screenplay as well as nominations for Best Director and Best Picture.

Asked what she planned to do next, Campion revealed she had long harboured the wish to bring to the stage Henry James's *The Portrait of a Lady*, in her opinion one of the top three novels of all time. It is the study of a spirited nineteenth-century young American woman trapped by the mores of her time. She also told a friend that she was considering approaching Nicole Kidman to play Isabel.

Henry James's book tells the story of Isabel Archer, a single-minded American heiress in Europe who turns down proposals of marriage from both her American and British suitors (played in Campion's film by Viggo Mortensen and Richard E. Grant) because she wants to explore life. But in Italy the apparently friendly Madame Merle (Barbara Hershey) steers her into a loveless match with manipulating, penniless artist Gilbert Osmond (John Malkovich).

Nicole, who had first read the book at seventeen, when it didn't mean much to her, and then again at twenty-two, by which time it meant more, duly flew to Australia and pleaded her case for five hours. But within a year Campion had changed her mind and decided she would prefer to film *The Portrait of a Lady* rather than stage it. The one snag was that she had got wind that Merchant Ivory was also planning a movie version of the novel.

Nicole, naturally, was still in Campion's thoughts to play Isabel Archer, and she was both heartened and, she says, 'quite shocked with her boldness' when Nicole called her to say that they should not worry about the rival version but should simply get on and make their own movie. Campion believes she would not have gone ahead if Nicole had not made that positively upbeat call.

Once the money to make the film was in place, Nicole could not wait to get started. But she was in for a severe shock. When Campion examined Nicole's recent movie track record, she saw nothing in it to give her confidence that the actress was capable of portraying the depths of depression and self-loathing Isabel endures while ensnared in an abusive relationship. Put bluntly, Campion did not think Nicole had the spirit for it after playing several 'Hollywood handbag' roles, as she dismissively labelled the sort of 'girlfriend' parts so many actresses have to put up with. The implication was that the actress had failed to protect her talent. To be fair, Nicole's problem was hardly of her own making. It was largely down to how she was perceived in Hollywood. As her *Batman Forever* director Joel Schumacher had astutely remarked: 'Nicole is a great character actress, with the body and face of a movie star.' At that point, however, Campion had not seen Nicole in *To Die For*, which showed the actress in a more complex and difficult role on the big screen than hitherto.

Campion had been planning to call Nicole about *The Portrait of a Lady* but Nicole telephoned her first and revealed herself to be in something of a crisis of faith over her acting career. She explained her dissatisfaction with some of the work she had been doing, said she felt like giving up acting, and intimated she was desperate to try something she really believed in. Nicole rightly saw Isabel Archer as the strong character role that could get her back on the acting track she had originally set out on and treasured most. When Campion expressed her doubts, saying some of Nicole's recent movies had not suited her, she then suggested that the only way her misgivings would be completely swept away would be if Nicole auditioned for the role. Jane has since admitted that this was a terrible thing to say to Nicole when she had previously told her she could have the part.

Predictably it brought an explosion of outrage from a sorely wounded Nicole. 'It was really hurtful at first,' she said, and a right royal row erupted between the two women. 'I became quite fiery, upset and emotional,' Nicole remembers. 'I yelled at

On the run from danger with George Clooney in *The Peacemaker*

Scary sisters: with Sandra Bullock in *Practical Magic*

(The Ronald Grant Archive)

Sympathetic wife to Michael
Keaton in *My Life*

(Rex Features)

Towering over husband Tom
Cruise in his
Top Gun-style shades

Seductive and sexy in *Eyes Wide Shut*

An intimate moment with husband Tom Cruise from *Eyes Wide Shut*

In spectacles, with eyes wide open

On stage in *The Blue Room*. One critic was moved to describe Nicole as 'pure theatrical Viagra'

In full voice with Ewan McGregor in *Moulin Rouge*

Showing a shapely leg as Satine in *Moulin Rouge*

Support from her
parents for newly single
Nicole at the Golden
Globe awards, 2002

A triumphant Nicole
with her Golden Globe
award

(Big Pictures)

Rallying round: actress
friends Naomi Watts
and Thora Birch

(Rex Features)

Sister Antonia was
Nicole's date at the
2002 Oscars

her and we had a terrible fight over the phone.' Campion felt such an eruption was, in the end, beneficial, a clearing of the air. In her opinion, by making quite plain how fed up and angry she was, Nicole brought a level of startling honesty to their relationship.

During two days of strenuous auditions in Los Angeles, Nicole and Jane forged their friendship anew, letting their hair down together and opening up to each other. Together they performed scenes from *The Portrait of a Lady* and tested each other out with improvisation, relaxation and, bizarrely, even some go-go dancing. By the end, Nicole had left her in little doubt that she had it in her to do justice to Jane and to the novel. Indeed she was desperate to do so. There was one obvious advantage for Jane Campion in casting Nicole as Isabel. Nicole's own transition from Australia to America could bear some comparison with Isabel's departing for Europe and being caught up in the machinations there. Nicole, more so perhaps than an American actress, might understand the role of having had to adapt swiftly at a young age to a new life and to different ways in a continent that was totally new to her.

There was one final hurdle. Nicole was warned she would have to wait for a full week before Jane would give her verdict on whether or not she would be Jane's Isabel Archer. Campion explained that she wanted time to examine the tape and that she would not be pressured into giving Nicole a premature answer. It was an agonising week of waiting for Nicole. She wanted the role so desperately it was gnawing away at her insides. Eventually Jane phoned her at home and said simply: 'You're my Isabel.'

Nicole dissolved into tears at the news. 'It was kind of like breaking my spirit and then putting it back together, which is

what happens to Isabel too. Jane likes her actresses to desperately, passionately want to be in her films and she likes to put
you through hard work to see if you have the stamina. I know
Holly [Hunter, who starred in *The Piano*] has a similar story.'

Together Jane and Nicole spent several weeks before filming
began, just exploring the core of Isabel's character and deciding
how they would together approach the film. Clearly it was
destined to be the most demanding of roles on all levels.
Intellectually complex, it would also require Nicole to be on
screen nearly all the time.

As Jane and Nicole reached deeper into Isabel's character,
they also became much more open with each other, sharing
secrets and thoughts, all of which contributed to a better
understanding between director and star. Gradually Nicole
found that working with Jane freed her up as an actress under
Jane's nurturing and encouragement as she sought to get right
inside Isabel's personality and her predicament of being a
woman incapable of escaping either emotionally or physically
an abusive husband. What particularly fascinated Nicole about
Isabel was that incapacity of leaving her husband despite the
emotional battering he constantly meted out to her. Isabel
hates the fact that she remains helplessly attracted to him, yet
she cannot find it in her to rid herself of that attraction and
break free.

Typically enthusiastic and detailed in her preparation, Nicole
read and re-read the Henry James book twice more and, to
enter its mood, listened to copious recordings by the soul-jazz
singer Nina Simone whose intensely personal and musically
bluesy laments about female oppression had made her a musical poet laureate of the sixties. Nicole also resolved to have
herself laced tightly into a corset every day to get the feel of

Isabel's hourglass figure. So tightly did she demand the knots be tied that by the end of the shoot the actress swore that her internal organs had shifted.

In those pre-production weeks Nicole spent alone with Jane Campion, the director began a process of 'stripping me of my mannerisms', as Nicole described them, or her 'little bag of tricks', and instilled in the actress her view of Isabel Archer as an intense and serious woman who had grown up with no sense of humour.

Nicole says she was terrified of meeting Malkovich because of his awesome reputation as an actor on both stage and cinema. Perhaps that was no bad thing in view of the relationship they were to have on screen. They were first brought together by Jane in a dusty old rehearsal hall in London. Nicole could see him sitting on a couch reading as she walked in and wondered how they would gell. Jane asked them to do some improvisation and Nicole found Malkovich every bit as impressive as she expected him to be.

The film would show three men in love with Isabel. John Malkovich, as the controlling husband, would be the one with whom Nicole would have the crucial, most compelling scenes. A full six weeks was set aside to shoot those scenes in Rome, most of which would be spent with Malkovich as Gilbert being emotionally abusive to Nicole's Isabel, while she still desperately tries to make him love her. Those six weeks would tax Nicole mentally in a way that she had never experienced on set before.

Emotionally it was a draining experience for Nicole to retire each night after Isabel's daily humiliations during which she shed real tears only to return early the next morning knowing she was to submit to more scripted offensive behaviour from her co-star. It was especially hard, she said, when she would get up at five o'clock in the morning ready to be in the make-up chair at 5.30 and then find that there was no hot water in the little villa she was staying in. Stepping into the shower and being jolted awake by the freezing water was enough of a shock to the system, but then thinking ahead to the trials that awaited her did not make for the easiest start to the morning.

Sometimes she did not altogether know everything that was coming. Malkovich, she noted, did a lot of unscripted things, too, including tripping her by standing on the hem of her dress and slapping her face with a glove which evoked responses from Nicole which, she says, surprised even her. It all, however, contributed immensely to the realism.

There is a scene in the movie, when Isabel's frustration boils over and she beats her head against the wall. Nicole swears it was a completely natural reaction on her part, something which just happened and was not planned. The first time she did it, Nicole simply was not conscious of it, but Jane Campion seized upon it as a wonderfully realistic reaction. Despite sporting a huge bruise on her forehead the next day, Nicole ended up doing more head-banging takes although the very first, the spontaneous one, was eventually chosen to be used in the final print.

Nicole emerged from the experience of playing Isabel Archer stating that she had learned a great deal from both Jane Campion and Henry James. Her admiration of Jane included praising her as 'a generous spirit, who has an enormous fascination with people and puts them on the screen in an original way'. At one point she had been worried that Isabel was being made to look so plain that she feared audiences would not believe Isabel worthy of their attention. But she had decided to trust Jane's judgement and the director had been proved right. From Henry James, Nicole believed she had learned specifically that it is all right to be emotional and vulnerable and to experience all those other feelings which lead you to a deeper understanding of yourself. Henry James, she pointed out, wrote that pain and suffering can teach you that you can deal with the situations that will arise. Nicole marvelled at James's ability to understand women's feelings and emotions.

The first time Nicole sat down with Jane Campion to watch the completed film she thought she was so terrible in it while everyone else was brilliant that she burst into tears. Then she watched it again and came to realise fully what Jane had accomplished and was proud of the movie as well as grateful to have been a part of it.

Nicole's performance provoked some talk of an Oscar nomination but, to her acute disappointment, the critics were divided over Campion's dark, modern interpretation of Henry James's story. Nicole, however, was at pains to point out that, because of the type of film it was, *The Portrait of a Lady* was not a movie which set out to please people, it was not asking to be liked. Besides, she revealed, Jane had told her that only ten out of every 100 readers really like the novel – it was a story that people either felt strongly about or did not understand.

The disappointment for Nicole was that many critics were unable to comprehend why Isabel does not simply walk away from her malevolent, cruel husband. She, however, could understand why some women were unable to extricate themselves from abusive situations in which, as one interviewer succinctly perceived it, there was a 'vicious circle of physical and emotional torment followed by a tenderness that characterises such relationships'. One favourite scene in the movie for

Nicole was when Osmond hits Isabel and pushes her to the floor and yet, once back on her feet, and with Osmond moving near as if about to kiss her, she is still reaching for him, still wanting him despite the abuse. Nicole felt this scene spelled out why Isabel stayed.

Notwithstanding the critics, the fact that Nicole had taken on the role at all had earned her enormous respect. Taking on Isabel made the American media sit up and regard her very differently from the actress who had played a dishy, decorative doctor in *Days of Thunder*, a femme fatale in *Malice* and a slinky sex kitten in *Batman Forever*. America's showbiz magazine *Entertainment Weekly* nominated Nicole as one of 'five savvy stars who got over their career slumps'. It added that *The Portrait of a Lady* proved 'she's willing to take a risk for art's sake'.

Jane Campion's parting words to Nicole were always to keep Isabel with her. She took that to mean that she should retain the experience of playing Isabel and remember what she had learned from it.

Once she had completed filming *The Portrait of a Lady*, Nicole felt so utterly exhausted both mentally and physically that she decided she would take six months off. She knew she was going to need the rest and a complete break before embarking on what she expected to be another truly remarkable experience – starring with husband Tom Cruise in Stanley Kubrick's first movie for ten years, *Eyes Wide Shut*.

In the event the film schedule for *Eyes Wide Shut* was delayed and, after she had gathered her strength and cleared her mind of Isabel Archer, Nicole was asked if she would find eight weeks in which to fit in a new movie called *Peacemaker*, also staring George Clooney. This was a nuclear thriller which was to be the debut movie of Dreamworks, the company formed by the triumvirate of Steven Spielberg, David Geffen and Jeffrey Katzenberg who had sunk their own money in the project in an attempt to attract further investment to set up what was effectively the first new major Hollywood studio in decades to make feature films, animation and TV shows.

The film was also the debut as a movie director of Mimi Leder, who had won an Emmy, television's equivalent of an Oscar, for her work on *ER* – hence her connection with Clooney. It was Mimi who cast Nicole. She said: 'I knew that her character is smart and precise in the way she goes about finding who the terrorist is, and that's how I saw Nicole: smart and precise, both in the way she tackles a role and the way she lives her life.' Clooney threw his weight behind Mimi's overtures to Nicole to come on board the movie, and because it was an action film, something she had not done before, she agreed.

Peacemaker offered Nicole the chance to play a dark-haired scientist called Dr Julia Kelly, head of the White House Nuclear Smuggling Unit, who teams up with Clooney as Lt Col Thomas Devoe, a maverick intelligence officer with Army Special Forces, to track down a stolen Russian nuclear device.

The unlikely couple are paired together after a train carrying nuclear warheads to be defused crashes somewhere in the Soviet Union. The train is wrecked in the nuclear blast to make it look as though all the warheads were destroyed by accident. But Devoe sees through the scheme and realises the bombs have been stolen and sold to terrorists. He and Dr Kelly fly over to wrest the warheads from the Bosnian terrorists to whom they were sold. But one detonator slips through the net and is smuggled into Manhattan, where the duo pick up the trail of the terrorist carrying his dangerous cargo in a backpack on the New York streets.

Clooney's character starts out making a fool of bureaucrat Nicole at a departmental briefing but their mutual dislike of each other dissolves into more complex emotions in the midst of the action. Nicole appreciated the fact that the pairing was a working relationship not a romantic one and that her character was not portrayed as a bumbling fool but as a woman who got more than her fair share of things right. Clooney commented: 'Nicole is just great. To play a government official and be a pretty girl, it's a tough sell. But she really does it.'

Nevertheless, to some observers it was still a surprising choice of movie for Nicole to make. But she gave a convincing and valid explanation. *The Portrait of a Lady* had been exhausting and on the horizon was *Eyes Wide Shut*. *Peacemaker* had simply looked like fun to her. She said: 'I was offered it right after *The Portrait of a Lady* and that was the hardest film I'd ever made – emotionally – so this was my way of going to have some fun. I wanted to be able to not have to work every day and to be able to go out at night and dance and go drinking with George. And that's what we did.'

After *Peacemaker* Nicole took another four months off with the children and spent the summer in Italy.

CHAPTER 12

✳

Eyes Wide Shut

'Nicole. Call me, I can't wait to talk to you'
— MESSAGE LEFT BY STANLEY KUBRICK
THE NIGHT BEFORE HE DIED

The first thing Nicole Kidman noticed about master film-maker Stanley Kubrick was his eyes wide open. The actress felt they looked right into her soul. 'They were the most extraordinary eyes I had ever seen in a human being,' she said. She was working in London in 1995 on Jane Campion's *The Portrait of a Lady* when the call from the great Stanley Kubrick came.

The call explained that Stanley Kubrick wanted to send her a script and a letter, and gave typically precise Kubrick instructions. Nicole should be at home at a particular time to receive them – to which she happily agreed. Not only that, she should be in as relaxed a frame of mind as she could summon when she first read the script. She should be rested and sitting comfortably. And afterwards she should call him and tell him what she thought. Nicole was in a state of some excitement by this stage. She knew and shared her husband Tom's opinion of Stanley Kubrick, who had not made a film since 1987 but whom both regarded as still the ultimate film-maker. She was also aware that Tom had been in touch with the great director about this new project. Kubrick was an admirer of Tom's acting, particularly of *Born on the Fourth of July*, and the two men shared an astonishing appetite for hard work. Tom had his own copy of the script delivered separately to him. Nicole had her own decisions to make.

She read the script which told the story of Dr William Harford and his wife Alice whose happy life together spirals into danger after a drug-fuelled row during which she confesses to fantasising about a handsome sea captain they once met. Stanley Kubrick's letter to Nicole explained that he would love her to play Alice. He thought she would be perfect in the role. Nicole agreed to visit the great man in person to discuss the project. But first she discovered from her agent that Kubrick had been calling for around nine months to see different tapes of her work. Her agent had not let her know because there had been no job offer at that time.

Nicole travelled the twenty miles from London to Stanley Kubrick's Hertfordshire home just outside St Albans with enormous trepidation. And her first impression was not a good one. 'I thought he was sort of scruffy,' Nicole laughs. But then she saw the extraordinary eyes. 'They are hooded eyes,' she said, 'and they have this wonderful mischievous quality, yet they also have this great sense of having lived.' The eyes bored into Nicole so deeply that she thought she was going to lose the part that was gradually becoming so important to her. She said she was convinced Stanley Kubrick was going to fire her before she even got started. That was something she very much did not want to happen, yet she said she was sure he was going to take a look at her and say, 'What was I thinking about?' Of course he did not. Stanley Kubrick thought Nicole Kidman was simply perfect as his Alice, just as he believed her husband Tom Cruise would be perfect as Alice's husband Bill. The deals were made and eventually, two years later, work started.

Eyes Wide Shut was based on a short novel by the Viennese playwright and physician Arthur Schnitzler called *Traumnovelle*. Stanley Kubrick had been fascinated by the powerful story of jealousy and sexual obsession for more than twenty years and had been striving for most of that time to find the perfect stars to bring it to the screen. He knew that in Tom Cruise and Nicole Kidman he had found them.

Schnitzler's novella was set in Vienna just over 100 years ago and centred on a married couple, a doctor called Fridolin and his wife Albertina. They were an attractive pair with a pretty young daughter but their relationship and indeed his life are threatened after they attend a masquerade ball. They are separately propositioned by other people but resist temptation and return home to make passionate love to each other. But Albertina idly admits that she dreamed of having sex with a man she met on holiday. The casual confession fuels a remarkable reaction in the doctor. He is deeply disturbed by thoughts of his beautiful wife's imagined adultery.

Later that night he is called out when a patient dies and is shocked to find the patient's distraught daughter suddenly announcing that she is in love with him. He calms her down, and after her fiancé arrives the doctor leaves and launches himself into a wild and emotional night. He visits a young prostitute to whom he is greatly attracted although he cannot complete the transaction. He lurches from there to meet up with an old friend who is a pianist heading for a bizarre engagement at a sophisticated orgy. The pianist is forced to play blindfold so that he cannot witness the debauchery which occurs.

In his confused state Fridolin is fascinated and persuades his friend to give him the password to get in. He has to acquire a costume and mask to wear to the occasion and finds himself involved in another moment of late-night titillation when he encounters the beautiful young daughter of the costumier.

He arrives at a grand house to take part in the elaborate orgy and the password enables him to enter. Inside he is shocked by the wild scenes of sexual abandon. Beautiful women are enthusiastically copulating with men in all variety of positions and places. But the atmosphere becomes hostile and one woman whispers a warning that he is in great danger. Before he can leave he is challenged by a group of the masked men who demand he gives the second password. When he fails he is exposed and threatened. But the woman who warned him steps forward and offers to take his place as a scapegoat.

Fridolin is whisked away and returns to his wife. But she is awakening from a dream and she further devastates the jealous husband by giving him graphic details of her sexual encounter with her imagined lover. Fridolin desperately tries to find his pianist friend to discover the truth of the previous night. But the musician has also been whisked away. And tragedy strikes when he learns that his beautiful and mysterious rescuer has died in deeply suspicious circumstances. As a doctor he is able to inspect the body.

Fridolin's life has been turned upside down by his reaction to his wife's apparently innocent confession that she was once strongly drawn to another man. Fridolin finally returns home to find his mask from the orgy lying next to Albertina in bed. He is horrified but he pours out his own confession to his wife and they are reconciled. Their marriage seems saved. She says she thinks they ought to be grateful that they have come unharmed out of their adventures, whether or not they were real, or only a dream. Fridolin is delighted to be happily reconciled but he does say darkly that: 'No dream is entirely a dream.'

For the difficult task of bringing Schnitzler's story up to the present day and eventually to the screen Stanley Kubrick contacted Oscar-winning writer Frederick Raphael in 1994. Their two-year collaboration is the subject of Raphael's captivating memoir, *Eyes Wide Open*. The project was conducted with Stanley Kubrick's legendary loving care and amazing attention to detail and the writers managed to create a brilliant script that contained warmth and humour as well as exploring the darker emotions. Schnitzler's story was changed and enhanced, Fridolin and Albertina becoming affluent Dr Bill Harford and his wife Alice and Vienna becoming New York, but jealousy and sexual obsession remained rigidly at centre stage.

The action begins as Bill Harford and his wife Alice head off to a glittering Christmas dance where they know hardly any of the guests. They are clearly a very attractive couple who are deeply in love with each other and devoted to their seven-year-old daughter. Bill spots an old friend who dropped out of medical school and is now playing piano with the band and stops to talk to him while Alice heads for the 'Ladies'. Bill is fascinated by his friend's story and Alice reaches for a little more champagne than she might normally have drunk as she waits by the bar for her husband. She starts dancing with a handsome older man with a heavy-handed seduction technique. Alice does not seem interested but allows herself to enjoy the dance. She spots her husband surrounded by a pair of pretty models, both evidently quite prepared to deliver themselves for full body examinations.

Bill is suddenly called to an emergency upstairs. A beautiful naked young woman has taken a drugs overdose and Victor, their embarrassed and half-dressed host, is anxiously hovering around. Bill helps the woman to recover and Victor is instantly deeply grateful. Bill and Alice return home and make love. It's a wonderfully sexy, romantic scene.

It impressed Stanley Kubrick so much that he was later to use it as the stunning teaser trailer for the movie, which shocked Tom Cruise. He said: 'It is one thing to be in a room with Stanley, doing that with your wife . . . but then suddenly it is up there on the screen.' But when he showed it to his mother and stepfather they were both impressed and when his mother said it was incredible and what a moving piece of work it was, Cruise relaxed a little.

The following morning the rich and successful doctor goes smoothly to work and even gives Nicole's mother a name check: 'Please ask Janelle if she would bring in my coffee.' That night Bill and Alice smoke a little pot together and look as if they are about to make love until a silly row breaks out. She admits that her dancing partner wanted to have sex with her. He says he did not sleep with the models because he is in love with her. She is stoned and accuses him angrily of only not going to bed with the models out of consideration for her. It's a key moment in the film because it changes the mood between them totally.

Alice is angry and confesses that she had vivid sexual fantasies about a young naval officer she saw on holiday the year before. He glanced at her in the hotel lobby and she could hardly move. She tells a horrified Bill that if the naval officer had wanted her, even for only one night, her desire for him was so strong that she was ready to give up everything, her marriage, her daughter and their future together.

It is a shocking and revealing scene. Kidman and Cruise are in their underwear in the bedroom as she lays bare this terrible secret that could shatter their characters' marriage. Nicole Kidman knew this screen moment was crucial to the whole movie. She explained: 'In the film after we have smoked pot we are so relaxed and careless talk threatens the marriage. That is what is so honest. Bill thinks he is going to have sex and we are set in for the night and he says one thing and it triggers a number of reactions from me and it is so real. It happens in marriages and relationships, Bill is reeling.'

Stanley Kubrick and his two stars debated the scene in enormous detail. In the painstaking Kubrick style every syllable of dialogue was carefully considered. 'Stanley would say that I ought to be a lawyer,' says Nicole, 'because I would debate each issue of the scene, each of the arguments.' She kept saying that every dangerous development of the row must be entirely logical and it was left to Kubrick to point out gently that Alice was stoned at this time so perhaps she was not thinking entirely straight. Nicole said Stanley reminded her that this was not a completely rational argument but an emotional outburst and people do say the most ridiculous things when they are arguing. In the end they loved the irrational edge to the argument and it is Alice's hysterical laughter that at one point drives her husband almost to distraction. The nudity involved did not bother Nicole because she was 'playing a character'. She said that people who imagined the film was going to be some kind of sex romp would be disappointed.

It is a powerful moment. Nicole is spellbinding as she delivers her bombshell, but although it is devastating for the husband, Nicole says: 'I think it is a very funny scene, I love Stanley's humour, and then Alice spews out things that she has held back for a long, long time.'

Bill is shattered, but before he can react he is called to the house of a patient who has died. As he races over there he has explicit fantasies of Alice making wild abandoned love to the naval officer. The fantasy scenes were especially difficult for Nicole to film, with Gary Goba who plays the officer. She said that she would not have gone quite so far with any other director. They were filmed over three days and, although she realised Kubrick wanted scenes which were almost pornographic, she did not feel exploited. She knew it was vital for the film for her husband to be driven half out of his mind by the thought of her with another man. Nicole said: 'The film deals with sex and sexual obsession and the scenes could not have been of me in a bra and panties pretending to have sex with somebody. It had to have a graphic quality to it. It was difficult going home to my husband after those scenes but we both decided we were basically going to get lost in this world for a year and a half and that is what we did.'

Bill arrives at his patient's home and as he is comforting the dead man's distraught daughter she suddenly kisses him passionately and says she loves him. Bill is shocked but just manages to calm the woman before her fiancé arrives and makes his escape.

Out in the streets of New York he is clearly in a different environment from his comfortable and safe home. A gang of drunks barge him off the pavement and jeer at him for being gay. He is approached by a beautiful young prostitute who takes him back to her flat. He agrees to pay the price but before he can complete the transaction he gets a telephone call from Alice. He explains he is still caring for his patient but the mood is broken with the prostitute. He pays her and leaves.

Walking along, still deeply troubled by Alice's earlier outburst, Bill sees a poster advertising Nick Nightingale, his old friend from medical school, and goes into a bar to hear him play. Over a drink his friend tells him he has to go on later to play at a bizarre engagement at a wild and sophisticated orgy. It is well paid but the event is secretly arranged and he has to play blindfold so that he cannot witness any of the indiscretions. Bill is instantly intrigued. In his current frame of mind an orgy seems like the most exciting idea in the world. Nick is waiting for a telephone call to give him the password to get in and the details of the venue. Bill bullies his friend into letting him in on the secret. But he has to wear a costume of a mask and cloak. With fantasies of Alice being ravaged by the naval captain flashing through his mind Bill becomes like a man possessed. He persuades a costumier to open up late at night, then takes a taxi to a huge country mansion. The password is Fidelio and it gets him past the burly security men. Inside he witnesses wild scenes of a sex orgy. Very attractive women are enthusiastically having sex with men all over the house. But before Bill can join in the action he is warned to leave by a beautiful naked woman.

Then suddenly he is approached by threatening heavies who

usher him inside a ring of clearly angry men wearing masks and cloaks. They challenge Bill to deliver the second password, and, when he fails, he is ordered to remove his mask. But before he can find out what his grisly fate is to be, the beautiful woman appears and insists she will take his place. Bill is ejected. He returns home to find Alice has just had a terrifying dream about being ravaged by the naval officer and lots of other men to try to make fun of her husband.

When he tries to find his friend again he has disappeared. He returns his costume but the mask is missing. He receives another warning to forget everything. And then the beautiful woman who came to his aid is found dead. The prostitute has been diagnosed with HIV and is missing.

Bill is shattered, and angrily confronts Victor who was one of the masked men. Victor insists it was an innocent charade but Bill furiously demands to know what sort of a charade ends with somebody dead. Victor threatens Bill and insists that he should forget about everything that has happened to him. Bill returns home to an even bigger shock – his missing mask is lying on the pillow next to sleeping Alice. He breaks down completely and tells her everything. The couple are forced into a blistering heart-to-heart that leaves them both emotionally exhausted. Alice particularly looks as if she has been crying for hours. When she asked how she achieved that level of realism, Nicole replied with a laugh: 'I cried for hours.'

At the end of the film Bill and Alice take their daughter Christmas shopping and seem determined to repair their relationship. He says that he wants them to be together forever, and she says that forever is a word that frightens. But Alice sets the seal on the nearest thing to a happy ending that Stanley Kubrick could devise when in the last line of the film she demands in the most graphic terms that her husband take her home and make love to her.

The level of intimacy between the two main characters was clearly the key to the success of the film. Tom Cruise and Nicole Kidman both knew that filming *Eyes Wide Shut* would mean exposing themselves both physically and mentally more fully than they had ever done before but they were both won over by the enthusiasm of Stanley Kubrick and the intensity of the remarkable script.

There followed one of the longest shoots in the history of cinema. For two years Tom Cruise and Nicole Kidman put themselves in the hands of the master in England in order to recreate a scenario in America that revealed a marriage shocked to its roots by the deepest and most painful feelings imaginable. It was one of the most fulfilling experiences of Nicole Kidman's life, yet she took some time to settle in to working with Stanley Kubrick. At first she was clearly in awe of his reputation and his towering intellect. Indeed for at least the first month of production she lived in daily fear of being fired. Nicole explained that Alice had two very long and important monologues which she thought would be so difficult to deliver that they would lead to Kubrick jettisoning her. 'I thought if he ever sees me doing those he is not going to want me in the film,' says Nicole.

She recognised afterwards that that was simply her insecurity as an actor, which was swiftly dispelled by working with Stanley Kubrick. He gave her such uplifting and insightful encouragement that her anxieties disappeared and she relaxed into one of the happiest experiences of her professional life. 'He gave me such confidence as an actor and really allowed me such freedom as an actor,' said Nicole. 'He would say, "OK, you've done a few takes, now you can do what you want to do." '

She had heard stories about Kubrick being incredibly controlling with his actors, demanding things were done in a precise and defined way but that was not how it felt to Nicole. 'At certain times he was very controlling but at other times not; he allowed me to just get lost in Alice and after a year and a half I just became that woman, in a weird way. I know that sounds ridiculous, but as an actor there is reality and there is pretend and those lines get crossed and you're working with a director who allows that to happen; it's exciting and dangerous – that's when the work becomes so much more than just making a film.'

Both Nicole Kidman and Tom Cruise found *Eyes Wide Shut* a huge and deeply intense experience. And although they were playing a couple going through the most traumatic examination of their relationship, they both insisted that it had made their real marriage stronger and closer. They were well aware that comparisons were inevitable between themselves and the rich and successful couple on screen with all their complex sexual hang-ups and fantasies. The scenes involving sexual jealousy and affairs with other partners were especially difficult. But both Nicole and Tom went into the project convinced that their own marriage was strong enough to withstand such goldfish bowl treatment and they trusted Stanley Kubrick implicitly.

Nicole said that she could not have imagined doing the film with anyone other than her husband, though she was delighted to take on the role with him by her side. She knew that there was an element of voyeurism in the movie and realised that was why Stanley Kubrick had wanted a married couple for the leading roles. She was well aware of how much she and Tom had put into the film. Many of the scenes were emotionally very harrowing. When questioned about the film at the launch Tom Cruise said: 'It could have destroyed our marriage but I think it has brought us together and we have this experience to remember for the rest of our lives. Nic and I have good communication but when you are dealing with the kind of issues that the film is confronting you really have to go through with it and discuss it. There are a lot of things we brought to the picture and I think Stanley appreciated it. I think he knew what it cost us to go through with these scenes. It was very demanding emotionally and physically for both of us and there were times when Nic and I were uneasy with each other. I think Stanley understood that and respected what we were doing and what we were giving.' Tom Cruise explained that he never brought his work home but because of the character and the nature of the scenes it was extremely hard not to think about it and become slightly obsessed with it.

He said that he had worked virtually every day on the movie, except when Nicole was filming the fantasy scenes with the naval officer, and sometimes the workload was hard on the two of them. 'We really had to take time to try and be good to each other and kind to each other. A relationship is something you always have to be creative in. I think Nic and I have learned that together. And this picture has given me a stronger belief in our friendship and our love.' Tom added that he was glad that they had been married as long as they had because *Eyes Wide Shut* would have been a great deal more difficult to make during the first year of their marriage.

Nicole was with her husband all the way on this theme and said: 'It came along at a time in our marriage when we were ready for it. We were both nervous because we were dealing with subject matter that is quite dangerous. But we had been married for seven years and we were willing to start talking about and dealing with things that a lot of the time you try to pretend are not there – desire, attraction to other people, all sorts of things. At times it was very difficult but we came out of it with our marriage strengthened because of the honesty it entailed.'

Making *Eyes Wide Shut* was clearly not an easy experience. It was two years out of their lives and Stanley Kubrick was certainly a most demanding director. He insisted on total secrecy about the project which helped to stir the media into a frenzy of curiosity. At one stage he even suggested that his stars should live apart to give more conviction to their characters. Yet Nicole felt privileged to have been part of the whole process. She loved the way Stanley Kubrick was always prepared to wait patiently for something to happen. He wanted a surprise and he was always so delighted when it came. Nicole loved it when she was able to surprise him. Kubrick's search for the perfect take was relentless but the number of takes he wanted did not bother her. In any case it was an unpredictable number. Sometimes he achieved what he wanted very quickly. And sometimes Nicole would startle him by herself asking to do another take.

'He made sure he discovered everything there was to discover,' said Nicole. She felt that so long as she was able to relax into the experience it was wonderful. There was no definite right or wrong to a performance, there were simply many facets to be explored. For the first time in her career Nicole really felt as if she was able to lose herself in her performance. She found she was constantly surprising herself. By being so close to both co-star and director she was really becoming Alice in what proved a magical, treasured experience. She had joined an elite club of actors who had enjoyed working with Stanley Kubrick and she felt that only those who had seen his passion for film at first hand could fully appreciate exactly what it was like to work with the great man.

Nicole loved the time spent living in London and working with Tom on the film. It was the longest she had spent in one place since she was a child and she felt safe and secure in spite of the ever-present interest of the press. They rented a lovely Nash house in Regent's Park and enjoyed holidays in the Lake District with their children. She was aware that audiences would watch the explicit sex scenes with an extra edge of interest because of the fact that she was with her husband, but she believed they were ready for the scrutiny. She found the whole film disturbing, though. It was that sort of movie.

Despite Kubrick's masterly direction and fine performances by his stars resulting in a relevant and riveting film, like many outstanding movies *Eyes Wide Shut* polarised opinion among the critics. Some loved it and some hated it.

Stanley Kubrick died shortly after he finished editing the movie. Both Tom Cruise and Nicole Kidman were devastated. She said: 'When I heard he had died my initial reaction was shock. I did not believe it and I did not want to believe it. He had so much to live for.'

She had spent a lot of time with Stanley Kubrick and he had become a sort of professional father figure for her. She said: 'I think it changed the way I view film-making. It gave me a belief in the art form of making film, however long it takes; it's extraordinary and wonderful. People view films in a very businesslike sort of way. We have a product and we've got to get it out. And film-making isn't that. It is about getting lost in that world and it is exquisite when it happens. Stanley Kubrick was someone who dedicated his life to films as an art form; he loved films and he lived films. Our great storytellers are so important and Stanley gave me a belief in that. He was one of the great storytellers of all time.'

The death of the director upset Nicole Kidman very deeply. She said that it tainted the whole wonderful experience. The night before he died Stanley Kubrick left a message saying: 'Nicole. Call me, I can't wait to talk to you.' She and Tom had watched the film together six days earlier and she had sat dumbfounded. Then she watched it a second time. Tom had expressed his approval but Nicole had lost her voice, so she had not had the chance to tell the director how much she liked it. She was cooking chocolate croissants for her children before phoning Kubrick when a call came through from his assistant to say that Stanley had sadly died. Nicole was distraught. Tom was in Australia while she was in New York. She called her husband and they both cried on the telephone. She could not stop crying for days. They flew to England for the funeral and Nicole was still terribly upset. She noted that Stanley hated funerals and she was surprised he had not banned the very idea, but it was an occasion for his widow Christiane and the family. Nicole said: 'I found it quite traumatic. I went to Princess Diana's funeral – Tom knew her, I had only met her a few times – but I had never been to a very intimate, private funeral.'

Nicole became very close to Stanley Kubrick and still feels the loss. She said: 'Stanley Kubrick was always encouraging to me as an actor and as a woman. The shock for Tom and me is that nobody knew us the way Stanley did. Not even my mum and dad. Nobody. It was three years with just the three of us. He knew us.'

CHAPTER 13

Divergent Careers

'At least I can wear heels again'
– NICOLE KIDMAN AFTER HER SPLIT
FROM TOM CRUISE

In January 2001 Nicole Kidman was forced to pull out of her next movie, *The Panic Room*, after just two weeks of shooting. She re-injured the knee she had hurt so badly when she took a fall while filming *Moulin Rouge*. Now it was proving too painful for her to continue. Nicole was to have played Meg Altman, a mother who tries to elude intruders who break into her house, and eventually seeks sanctuary in a 'panic room' designed to keep her from harm. Withdrawing from the movie was a bitter blow for Nicole, but it paled into insignificance compared with what was in store for her in a year which would turn her life upside down.

Weeks later, on 5 February 2001, Nicole and Tom's high-powered publicist Pat Kingsley issued the following statement which stunned Hollywood and reverberated around the world.

TO: Whom It May Concern
FR: Pat Kingsley
RE: Tom Cruise and Nicole Kidman

Tom Cruise and Nicole Kidman announced today that they have regretfully decided to separate. The couple who married in 1990 stressed their great respect for each other both personally and professionally. Citing the difficulties inherent in divergent careers which constantly keep them apart, they concluded that an amicable separation seemed best for both of them at this time.

The couple's marriage break-up inevitably made headlines on TV and in newspapers around the world, accompanied by speculation, mostly wild, as to why Hollywood's golden couple had split up. One theory was that Tom had fallen for Penelope Cruz, the co-star of his latest movie *Vanilla Sky*. But there was genuine shock at the announcement since Nicole and Tom had given the impression that theirs was one of the most solid marriages in Hollywood. 'Nic and I are forever,' Tom had often said. And Nicole had frequently declared she confidently expected to be with Tom well into their old age.

An examination of the couple's respective schedules since their fifteen months together on *Eyes Wide Shut* certainly pointed to 'divergent careers'. In 1998 Tom had worked on *Magnolia*, for which he was nominated for an Oscar, then spent the first half of 1999 making *Mission: Impossible 2*, followed by a tour of twenty countries to promote the movie in the middle of 2000. Then, in November 2000, he teamed up again with his

Jerry Maguire director, Cameron Crowe, to film *Vanilla Sky* in Los Angeles and New York.

Nicole, meanwhile, had filmed *The Birthday Girl* in Sydney and London and from October 1999 to May 2000 worked on *Moulin Rouge*, before moving on to Spain for three months making *The Others*.

For both Tom and Nicole it had undoubtedly been a hectic few years. All through their marriage, they had taken measures to avoid the long separations which so often are the cause of the break-up of Hollywood couples. 'We haven't been separated for more than twelve days,' said Tom in 1999. Nicole, for her part, had spoken of the need for them both to nurture their relationship. 'If that means talking on the telephone for two hours when you're extremely tired, you do it. But that doesn't mean giving up your goals and your career. All it means is pushing yourself a little harder.' Now their separation statement was indicating that they, too, had fallen victim to 'divergent careers'. Two days after the shock announcement of their split, it became apparent that it was irrevocable. Tom Cruise filed for divorce on the grounds of irreconcilable differences.

Within days of the announcement that the fairytale marriage was over, Nicole's mother Janelle and her sister Antonia with her two children flew into Los Angeles to join Nicole at her Pacific Palisades home. Cruise had moved out to the luxury Bel Air hotel in Beverly Hills.

For Nicole, Janelle and Antonia's rapid response to her woes was much needed. She always felt most comfortable when surrounded by her family and their swift arrival to offer support, warmth and loyalty meant so much to her. Her closest friends, including actress Naomi Watts, also instantly rallied round to provide a shoulder to cry on when needed. Naomi even moved into Nicole's house to be with her. Other close friends who were frequently on hand to cheer her up included a physical therapist and an acting teacher. Later Rebecca Rigg, another long-standing actress friend, also moved into Nicole's home. Comfortingly for Nicole, she was far from alone during this desperately difficult period. The house was filled with women and children, a real family atmosphere which helped to lift her spirits.

There was widespread public sadness for Nicole at the revelation that her seemingly idyllic marriage was over. But that was nothing compared with the wave of public sympathy for her when it was revealed that she had suffered the heart-ache of a miscarriage on 16 March.

It was later confirmed that Tom Cruise was the father. It was the saddest of ironies that Nicole should have been pregnant just as they were separating after both had expressed many times their deep desire to have a child together. Of her family, Nicole had often said she felt two children were enough but that she would love to give birth to a child of her own.

Soon the world was given an insight into the final days of the marriage. In a written response to the divorce petition filed by Cruise, Nicole said she had been shocked when the actor told her he no longer wanted to be married. The nine-page legal document lodged with the Los Angeles Superior Court revealed:

On Sunday 4 February, 2001, (Cruise) told (Kidman) that he no longer wanted to live with her and that he wanted a divorce. (Kidman) protested (Cruise's) intention to dissolve their marriage and urged him not to leave, but to enter marriage counselling with her, or to take other steps to address whatever problems may have existed in their marriage relationship. (Cruise) said his decision was final, and he departed the parties' home.

This came as a shock to respondent (Kidman). On 24 December 2000, the parties had happily celebrated their tenth anniversary with a group of friends. During the balance of December and thereafter, the parties were intimate; in fact (Kidman) became pregnant by (Cruise) but lost the baby through a miscarriage.

In the papers lodged by her lawyers Nicole followed Tom's lead and requested a dissolution of their marriage, citing irreconcilable differences. She asked for joint custody of the children and confirmed she wanted to continue her acting career.

(Kidman) intends to make her best efforts to continue her career in the performing arts, subject to limitations imposed upon her by reason of (i) the need for her to care for the children and to safeguard their emotional wellbeing; and (ii) the recent serious injury to her knee.

This was a reference to Nicole's fall in *Moulin Rouge*.

On top of trying to come to terms with such a devastating, traumatic blow as losing a baby, Nicole had to face up to what was now shaping up to become a tricky divorce. Tom Cruise was estimated by *Fortune* magazine to be worth around $250 million. And although the legalities of ending the marriage were proceeding to a conclusion, a settlement trial dealing with the dispersal of their properties around the world, cash, aeroplanes and jewellery was looming.

Also looming for Nicole was the 7 August premiere in Los

Angeles of her latest movie, the supernatural thriller *The Others*, which, coincidentally, had Tom as executive producer. Both Nicole and Tom had, of course, been expected to attend. But, by an extraordinary trick of fate, the premiere was scheduled for the very last day Tom and Nicole would officially still be man and wife. At 12.01 a.m. on Wednesday 8 August, the divorce of Nicole Kidman and Tom Cruise would become final.

There was therefore much feverish speculation as to whether Nicole and Tom would both attend the premiere and, if they did so, who would accompany them. By now it had been confirmed that Cruise was dating the beautiful dark-haired Penelope Cruz.

The premiere was a typically glitzy, star-studded Hollywood affair. But this time the massed ranks of TV crews, photographers and reporters, as well as a large crowd, were there with one purpose – to observe how the actor and actress who had been Hollywood's golden couple for ten years would spend their final married hours.

Nicole was the first to arrive at the Directors Guild of America's screening auditorium, quickly joined by Naomi Watts and Rebecca Rigg and Alejandro Amenabar, director of *The Others*. In a slinky, strapless black dress and high, high heels, Nicole looked composed and showed a very brave face.

About twenty minutes later, Tom showed up alone and evaded questions on the red carpet about the marriage or Penelope Cruz. 'I think she's very good in this movie,' he said gallantly of Nicole, adding he had told her precisely that. 'I am glad he is here to support the movie,' said Nicole equally gallantly. But they gave each other a wide berth and, after the screening, Tom disappeared telling reporters it was his turn to look after the kids while Nicole went on to the premiere party.

That night *The Others*, with Nicole Kidman as its leading lady, was launched on the way to a staggering box office return of over $100 million. It was to surpass everyone's expectations and elevate her to a new level of bankability as a movie star. As everyone associated with the film toasted its success at the party, the clock ticked around to midnight, a new day dawned, and Nicole Kidman was no longer Mrs Cruise. It was official.

Despite this legal severance, ahead still lay the settlement trial which was set for 4 October. In the event, it was delayed because both sides could not work out a deal. Negotiations continued because neither wanted a public hearing about who was getting precisely what and about arrangements regarding the children.

The most crucial argument centred on exactly when the couple had split, either just before their tenth wedding anniversary in December (Cruise's version) or in February (Nicole's). Under Californian law, the date had a dramatic effect on Nicole's entitlements. She took steps to prove they had been intimate after their anniversary and that the baby she had miscarried was Tom's.

Then, on 15 November, in an unscheduled court appearance in Los Angeles, the couple's lawyers presented a confidential document to Judge Lee Smalley Edmon that brought the divorce battle to an end. Cruise's lawyer, Dennis Wasser, confirmed that a deal had been reached but that the details would remain secret after Judge Edmon sealed the court file. The out-of-court settlement effectively meant that the threat of the couple's disagreements descending into a bitter public court squabble was averted.

Wasser and Nicole's lawyer, Sorrell Trope, released a joint statement stating that the couple have come to an amicable, full resolution of all issues. This was done to ensure that the best interests of the children were protected. The terms and conditions of their agreement are confidential. The parties will remain close friends.

According to *People* magazine, the hard-fought settlement was sealed with a little hug between Nicole and Tom. The couple shared custody of the children who would live with their parents alternately. Nicole kept the $20 million mansion in Los Angeles and the $10 million eight-bedroom harbour front three-storey villa at Darling Point, Sydney. Tom kept the aeroplanes, including his beloved Gulfstream IV jet, which boasts three bedrooms and a fitted kitchen. He also kept the $10 million estate in Telluride and their $11 million New York apartment.

Just hours after the finalisation of his divorce, Tom appeared on American TV declaring that he still loved Nicole. In the interview, recorded earlier in the week, he revealed: 'I have learned a lot about myself, that change is not a bad thing and that sometimes you have to confront things for everyone. I feel that you can get through things and you can still love that person and care about people even if you have disagreements – and I feel that way about Nic.'

He added: 'What I had with Nic, we had some extraordinary moments together and times that I will cherish and never forget.' He was also quoted as saying: 'We have always been a family. Even though the parents are no longer together, we still care about each other. We are going to raise these kids together, Nic and I.'

In the remaining weeks and months of 2001 Tom would frequently be pictured with Penelope Cruz by his side. It was clear that they were becoming ever closer. Just as had happened with Nicole on *Days of Thunder*, the actor had fallen for the beautiful young co-star of his latest film.

Nicole, meanwhile, was, absurdly, romantically linked to Russell Crowe after they happened to be in Fiji together. The Aussie-based Oscar-winning actor has known Nicole for many years and they have never been more than just extremely good friends. On this occasion he was simply passing through Fiji after completing filming on his latest movie *A Beautiful Mind*, while Nicole was there taking a well-earned holiday.

Gradually there were signs that she was coming to terms with the end of her marriage. In a revealing interview with Britain's top chat-show host Michael Parkinson, Nicole managed not to mention Tom Cruise once by name. But she did reveal how much she had been hurting.

'Divorce is divorce,' she said. 'It's my journey, I didn't expect it to happen to me, and it has happened, and it's a really tough thing to go through and it leaves you shaken and your whole foundation is sort of a mess and then you have to pick yourself up and move forward. And that's what I'm doing. You have two kids and there's times when you say "I just want to curl up in bed" and then you have a six-year-old coming in and going "Where's breakfast?" '

Despite the bitter divorce, Nicole said she still treasured romantic memories of the times she shared with Tom. 'I spent eleven years with him and there's something strangely romantic about being very well known and being together which people don't understand because you're in a fish bowl. But you also only have each other because nobody else really understands. So you have this kind of cocoon, a bubble that you exist in together and that's quite romantic. I mean I'm a romantic so I love anything like that.' She added that she would love to get married again.

Speaking of the strain of being married to such a famous movie heart-throb, she revealed: 'We would go to Rome and he wouldn't want to walk down the street during the daytime, or couldn't walk down the street in the daytime because of people coming up. So we would see cities at night. We'd break out of the hotel room and run around at three in the morning and just do it that way. We broke into the Colosseum! We climbed the fences and broke in. It's a way of dealing with being really well known but still being able to see a city like Rome.' Nicole had lived in the city when making the film *An Australian in Rome* early on in her career and she said: 'I knew it quite well. But he'd never been there and I wanted him to see it, and we saw it by moonlight.'

In every interview Nicole paid tribute to her mother and father who were pulling her through with love, devotion and advice. 'As my dad said, "Nic, it is what it is, it's not what should have been, nor what it could have been, it is what it is," ' she said. Janelle had always taught her that she would be able to hold her head high if she had conducted herself properly and she was able to do just that.

Commendably, Nicole washed no dirty linen in public. Her uppermost thoughts were for her children. 'Tom and I will be the parents of two children for the rest of our lives and that is the priority,' she said. 'So with that comes the need to be very mature and the need to deal with it rationally. My success was always going to be my marriage, so I suppose in my eyes I am not successful at all. If my kids tell me in ten years time, "Mummy, you raised us the best way you could and we're very proud of you," then I will feel a success.'

Nicole had been twenty-two when she first met and fell for Tom Cruise. She was rising thirty-four when the marriage came to an end and, with the certainty of hindsight, she could see how much she and Tom had changed. She may have thought she was worldly wise at twenty-two having travelled extensively, but she could not possibly have known what it would be like to be married to a megastar like Tom.

There was a time when her affair with Tom was in its first full flush of passion when she suddenly had an inkling of what she had let herself in for. While making the movie *Far and Away* she and Tom were renting a coastal cottage in Ireland and together they would ride their bicycles to the shore for romantic isolated walks along the beach. But one evening, after a day's filming, Nicole made her way to the barriers manned by security men to keep back inquisitive onlookers and found 200 girls screaming their heads off deliriously for Tom Cruise. She was astounded.

Soon baseball caps and sunglasses became *de rigueur* for the couple if they were to avoid the stares, the requests for autographs, the screams and the fan worship, although Tom's sunglasses invariably still tended to give him away as he had worn them to some effect in *Risky Business* and *Top Gun*.

Looking back, Nicole can see that, at twenty-two, she too was simply mad for Tom Cruise. She was a young woman following her heart, overwhelmed with love for Tom and she could barely believe it when it was reciprocated. She believed he was just the right man for her and her love for him was so consuming that, having treasured her independence so fiercely, she was even prepared to abandon her home in Australia literally on the spot. She called Antonia and told her to move into the apartment she had been so proud to have managed to buy for herself by the time she was twenty. 'I left my flat in Australia and never went back. I kind of went, "Oh, forget my career, who cares?" Suddenly I was going, "No, no, no, forget that – I just want to be married and have kids," and I allowed myself to be defined by a man and that was OK. I wanted that.'

In the eleven years they were together Nicole and Tom taught each other much. Nicole, not least, coaxed workaholic Tom to pause and smell the roses – literally. She proved a keen gardener at their Pacific Palisades home. She gave him an appreciation of Italian culture and the history of art and he brought out the athletic daredevil adventurer in her, introducing her to go-karting, rock climbing, skiing, aerobatics, sky diving and scuba diving.

Those looking for clues for the break-up of their marriage pointed to the couple's nomadic lifestyle. When they got bored in one place or when work called, they would pick everything up, plus of course the children, and move somewhere else. With homes around the world they were able to do so without too much trouble but some observers felt that such shifting sands ultimately proved unsettling. Nicole admits she loves it when the telephone unexpectedly rings to tell her she will be needed in another country in a couple of months. It appeals to her impetuous streak and she enjoys working out the logistics of making the move.

Eleven years together as a couple can almost be regarded as a successful union in Hollywood circles. And while they were a loving couple, the tales of Tom and Nicole's devotion to each other were numerous. They were so openly adoring of each other on the set of *Far and Away* that one member of the production team said he felt like throwing a bucket of water over them.

In one legendary declaration of love apparently Tom flew Nicole in his private jet to Paris from Los Angeles and thence to Versailles. A luxurious hotel room was not enough for his lady love – Tom had hired a room at the Palace of Versailles and the couple were greeted by a string orchestra playing Vivaldi, rose petals strewn over the floor, and a regally ornate table laid for two in a room steeped in history. There they ate, drank and danced till dawn. The story only added to the image of a fairytale marriage.

Nicole has conceded that having voluntarily given herself so completely over to Tom, her career was bound to suffer. 'I was married to Tom and he was doing these extraordinary roles and I just felt like such a loser,' she said on TV in Australia. She added: 'I said halfway through the marriage "I don't want this now, I want your influence but I kind of want to find out who I am."'

Once her film promotional duties were finished in 2001, Nicole revelled in spending more time with her children. She thoroughly enjoyed devoting hours to Isabella and Connor which, before they came along she reserved for herself, even if it did mean she did not read a book for six months whereas she used to get through at least one a week. 'It's amazing the way my life has twisted and turned,' she said. 'I used to take my hat off to any woman who is a single mother – and now that person is me.'

There were times when Nicole felt the upheaval that had occurred in her life, coupled with the scrutiny and speculation, was all just too much to handle, but at other times she knew she could deal with it. She said she saw herself as a Sydney girl, working as an actress, who has a completely overwhelming life that has evolved and happened. 'I'm moving on with my life.

I've been talking about me and Tom for a year but I have come out of it stronger,' she concluded.

It was ironic that Nicole's personal low-point should have occurred around the time when her standing as an actress – both on stage and screen – had probably never been higher. It had reached an altogether different level after she daringly agreed to star in the erotic play *The Blue Room* at London's Donmar Warehouse, in which her performance was famously described by one London critic, Charles Spencer of the *Daily Telegraph*, as 'pure theatrical Viagra'.

The Blue Room was based on the play *La Ronde* by Arthur Schnitzler and it had a chequered history. Vienna police had closed down its first public performance in 1921 and prosecuted Schnitzler for obscenity. It had been freely adapted for the London stage by David Hare, and starred Nicole and British actor Iain Glen playing five couples in a daisy-chain of brief sexual encounters set in London.

Because of the play's content – there would be one brief moment of nakedness for Nicole where she would be seen nude from behind for fifteen seconds – it was a controversial career move for the actress, viewed with incredulity by some close to her that she should agree to appear in 'some silly fringe theatre' for the most modest of wages when she was such a famous film star.

In fact, the production nearly did not go ahead when Nicole got cold feet – not because of the nudity but because of her fear of not being able to grasp the English accents required for her roles as a prostitute, a sophisticated English woman, a cocaine-snorting model and an actress. She worked hard with a dialect coach but still felt unsure enough to call the director, Sam

Mendes, in something of a panic. She feared her English accent would not be convincing enough for an English audience.

Nicole's crisis of confidence came one night when she was alone in a London hotel room, tossing and turning – and fretful. She decided she simply could not go on, and called first Tom Cruise, in tears, asking how she could get out of it. Tom told her she could not and she would not. She would be fine, he said. Still tearful, she then called her dad who talked her through her fears for fully forty-five minutes and set her mind at rest. Heartened by his sensibly reasoned encouragement, Nicole told herself that she was willing to fall flat on her face and that if *The Blue Room* did not work out then it was just one of those things.

Quite simply, though, Nicole was a sensation. *The Blue Room* played to packed houses from 22 September to 31 October 1998 and elicited universal rave reviews for the actress who played all five of her roles in minimal figure-hugging outfits. All the sex scenes were in blackout with a caption drily informing the audience of how long each coupling lasted.

Aside from memorably dubbing the play 'pure theatrical Viagra', Charles Spencer in the *Daily Telegraph* informed his readers that Nicole was 'achingly beautiful', 'drop-dead gorgeous' and 'bewitchingly adorable'. He could hardly have been more enthusiastic about Nicole. 'The vision of her wandering around the stage with a fag in one hand and her knickers in the other as a delicious French au pair will haunt my fantasies for months,' he drooled. Spencer said: 'Kidman is also a terrific actress who brings all five of her roles to instantly distinctive life, whether she's playing a cheap tart, a sophisticated married woman, a coke-sniffing waif of a model or a femme fatale of an actress.'

Nicholas de Jongh in the *Evening Standard* said: 'Miss Kidman lacks much theatrical experience. But all five roles are in her elegant, confident grasp.' Michael Billington in the *Guardian* began his review with: 'Yes, Nicole Kidman can certainly act.' He went on to say she was 'a superb character actress' and added: 'Kidman switches personae with consummate ease. She is not just a star, she genuinely delivers the goods.'

Thirty-eight-year-old Iain Glen, who had the enviable task of playing Nicole's five lovers, claimed that the sexual atmosphere they created on stage was never an issue with their respective spouses. 'Tom and I didn't really have a conversation about these scenes,' said Glen who was required to display more nudity on stage than Nicole. 'He didn't say: "Hey, you're kissing my wife," and the fact that he was in the audience didn't bother me or him or my wife.

'Nic and I got on very well. The truth is that you're just trying to do what's required in a scene. And if you need to be very much in love, or in lust with each other, or take your clothes off, then that's what you do.' Glen became friendly enough with both Tom and Nicole for the couple to invite him to America to stay at their house.

After seven weeks of stunning success at the Donmar Warehouse where the audience contained a strong contingent of celebrities every night, *The Blue Room* moved to New York to the Cort Theater on Broadway from 13 December to 4 April 1999.

Again it was hailed as a triumph for Nicole and she won glowing notices. As in London, her nude scene warranted much attention in the press and American magazines even went so far as to print diagrams of where members of the audience should sit at the Cort Theater to see more than just a bare Kidman bottom.

The Blue Room had been a gamble for Nicole, but it paid off handsomely. Her cachet as an actress increased dramatically, and *Moulin Rouge*, quickly followed by the remarkable success of *The Others*, went a long way to making up for some of the lacklustre movies she had recently been associated with, such as the comedy-romance *Practical Magic*, in which she starred with Sandra Bullock as two spooky sisters in a family of witches. Sandra played the straight sister, Nicole played the wild, sexy, tattooed, chainsmoker.

The Blue Room proved that Nicole was now ready to follow her instincts and throw herself into projects she believed in regardless of the size of the fee. She had never been short of offers of movie roles. Indeed she had reportedly turned down the leads in *Elizabeth*, which won fellow Aussie actress Cate Blanchett a Golden Globe award, *The Avengers*, which was taken up by Uma Thurman, and *Entrapment*, which gave Catherine Zeta Jones another leg up the Hollywood ladder. Some roles Nicole turned down in order to spend more time with her family, but it was the really interesting, not necessarily mainstream, female roles she was prepared to wait for.

Soon, she followed through on another interesting movie offer, playing a Russian mail order bride for a stuffy Englishman in *The Birthday Girl*, directed by Jez Butterworth. Typically, Nicole began studying Russian to bring some authenticity to the part.

After the traumatic split from Tom Cruise, a role in the film *The Others*, about a mother who has an obsessional love for her two children and is desperate to protect them because they are special needs children, hardly seemed the ideal vehicle for an emotionally battered Nicole to move on to. But she was

committed to starring in the movie, a chilling tale of psychological terror to be directed by young Chilean-born, Madrid-
based Alejandro Amenabar.

The director had written the story himself, about a young
woman called Grace on the island of Jersey, fourteen miles off
the coast of Normandy, who is waiting for her beloved husband to return from the front in the final days of the Second
World War. Grace has been raising her two young children
alone in a beautiful, but cavernous Victorian mansion. The
children are allergic to light and, although the house is of
necessity dark with shutters and curtains drawn, it is the one
place Grace believes them to be safe. But they are not.

When three new servants arrive to replace the ones who
have inexplicably left, startling supernatural events begin to
happen. Grace's daughter reveals she has been communicating
with unexplained apparitions. At first Grace is reluctant to
believe in her children's frightening sightings, but soon she too
begins to sense that ghostly intruders are at large. Who are
they? What do they want from Grace and her family? It
becomes apparent that the house is haunted by unseen pres-
ences. Grace, a devout Catholic, turns to her faith when her
life starts to fall apart. But in order to discover the truth, she
must abandon her fears and her Christian beliefs and enter the
otherworldly realm of the supernatural.

It was the religious aspect of *The Others*, Nicole admits, which
drew her to the role of Grace. 'I was raised a very strong
Catholic,' she explained, 'and still have huge elements of
Catholicism in me. It's a film about beliefs and at the end says,
"I don't know I'm wiser than you." Her whole foundation gets
rocked.'

Amenabar knew the key to his movie would be the actress

who plays Grace. To capture Grace's journey he needed an actress capable of embodying a roller-coaster range of emotions from maternal love to creeping paranoia to shattering shock. He also wanted an actress with classical grace, a sophisticated headstrong woman for whom a supernatural experience would be the last thing she expected – an experience that begs the question for her of who to trust, what to fear and what to believe.

'What really drew me and captured me completely about Nicole was the undeniable force of her stare,' said Amenabar. 'Much of the terror created in the film takes place in Nicole's eyes. They are better than any special effects money can buy.'

The movie required Nicole to decamp to Spain. The fog-swathed exteriors of an old English-style manor would be filmed in Cantabrie, a city on the misty Atlantic coast of Spain, and the interiors were to be specially created on a soundstage in the middle of suburban Madrid. There, Amenabar created a spooky house of long corridors, grey shades, shifting shadows and other unsettling effects.

Nicole arrived in Spain a week earlier than she needed to. When she sat down and re-read the script and realised what she was up against she wanted to back out. 'I really tried to get out of the movie,' she said. 'I even came up with a list of other actresses who could do it. When I arrived in Spain I and every part of me, every cell in my body, was saying No. I couldn't sleep. Roles affect me. I was terrified, I thought my kids wouldn't forgive me, that it was a sin to be doing it. It was the most extreme reaction I've ever had. For *The Blue Room* I just had the fear of doing theatre. But this was a physical reaction against the themes of the movie. Everyone kept telling me this put me in the right mood.'

Stoically Nicole got on with the job and put her trust in Amenabar. 'He was not afraid to go to the very darkest places, and he gave me the courage to go there with him as Grace slowly begins to accept that reality is not quite what she thinks it is.'

When it was released, *The Others* was hailed as one of the best films about ghosts ever, and it had audiences flocking to see it. Nicole was thrilled, although she likened the movie's resounding commercial success as forbidden fruit for her. 'I was in *Batman Forever*, but I've never had my movie be a hit movie before,' she explained. 'It's lovely because it gives me the power now to do something else that's a little bit offbeat and they'll finance it.

'Strangely enough, I thought "I'm making this strange atmospheric thriller that's got these dark undertones." I've always described it as a genre picture with a female lead that has undertones of Greek tragedy. It plays as just a thriller, and as a film which has other layers. It's about obsessional love and the way she obsessionally loves these children and is driven by protecting them. She loses her husband and it's all left on her shoulders. I really felt for her and said, "This must not be a film in which the mother is judged too severely." I wanted her to be someone you can feel for. And it all comes from her desire to be a good mother.'

CHAPTER 14

Diamonds, Satine and Lace

'She sings, she dances, she dies'

– BAZ LUHRMANN

While Nicole Kidman was wowing audiences nightly on Broadway in *The Blue Room* in the winter of 1998, one night she received backstage one dozen long-stemmed red roses from an ardent admirer. But this was no gift from a besotted fan or a stage door Johnny. The roses were an enticing offering from colourful Australian film director Baz Luhrmann, a long-time enthusiast of Nicole's work, who had attached to the roses a note which read: 'I have this great character for you. She sings, she dances, and then she dies.'

Nicole had known Baz for many years through their Australian film industry connections, and when she followed up his intriguing note it marked the start of a remarkable eighteen-month journey for them both which was to result in *Moulin Rouge.*

At that stage, Baz had just an outline for the musical he was planning about the most legendary nightclub of them all, the Moulin Rouge, founded in Paris in 1889. 'When I met with him, he didn't have a script,' Nicole remembers, 'but he had his book full of ideas, pictures, drawings of what he kind of wanted, the feel and atmosphere of the movie and the story.'

The character who sings, dances and then dies, explained Baz, was the most beautiful courtesan in Paris. She was called Satine, the star attraction at the Moulin Rouge, who has an ill-fated love affair with an impoverished poet. But, Baz stressed to Nicole, the story was not set in stone and it would evolve and change due to the work they would do prior to shooting. Baz also stressed he would need a six-month commitment from Nicole before the actual shoot. That was his film-making process, he said, take it or leave it. Oh, and there was just one more thing, he added smiling persuasively. The good news was that the movie would be shot in Sydney, the bad news was that he would require Nicole to audition for the role!

Nicole's initial reaction was to tell Baz that he had got the wrong girl. But his wholehearted enthusiasm for the project was highly infectious and, knowing Baz as she did, *Moulin Rouge* was going to be no ordinary screen musical. Like other Australians in the entertainment industry, Nicole had noticed the director first make his mark in Sydney with his production of *La Bohème* for Opera Australia. It had attracted wide praise for its originality and innovation.

It was only natural that he would then want to bring his natural flair to the movies – his parents had run a cinema as well as a farm and a service station in Herons Creek, the little town on the New South Wales mid-north coast where Baz was brought up.

Luhrmann's first feature film, *Strictly Ballroom*, turned out to be a remarkably confident debut, a bright, breezy and immensely likeable musical comedy about a young dance star who wants to break the rules and the opposition he faces from the ballroom dancing establishment. The movie made millions, and Baz then went on to totally reinvent the Shakespeare film with a thoroughly modern take on *Romeo and Juliet*. His unique interpretation of Shakespeare's timeless tale included setting his version in the mythical city of Verona Beach with Leonardo DiCaprio and Claire Daines as the star-crossed lovers playing out their doomed love affair in a dazzling modern world to a contemporary rock music backbeat. But, as he embarked on *Moulin Rouge*, Baz was aware that recent cinematic history was against him and that it was littered with instances of very good directors who had stumbled when it came to making musicals.

Nicole had never shown herself to be a singer in any previous movie, apart from her role in *Windrider* at the age of seventeen when she portrayed budding rock star Jade Kelly. In a *Sixty Minutes* TV documentary she had been shown with the family gathered round the piano enjoying a sing-song at home, but no one could recall her singing on film. However, she had always enjoyed music, and although she had given up her ballet lessons fairly young, she loved dancing and was never slow to get up on the dance floor.

For her audition Nicole chose to sing 'Nobody Does It Better' from *The Spy Who Loved Me* and then, daringly, she went into 'Diamonds Are a Girl's Best Friend'. This was the song which Marilyn Monroe had breathily made so uniquely her own in the

1953 movie *Gentlemen Prefer Blondes* and Baz was planning to include it in his movie. That was some challenge for Nicole! Baz had already heard her sing a little in *The Blue Room* and he was in no doubt that she could carry off the role of Satine. Her considerable acting skills were proven, she had innate style and as an actress she knew how to make an entrance.

Cast alongside her was Scottish actor Ewan McGregor as Christian, the poet who falls hopelessly in love with Satine. Ewan had a creditable baritone voice but he and Nicole were under no illusions. Realising the enormity of the project they were taking on and the weight of responsibility on their shoulders, the two stars made a pact that they would be willing to take risks and make complete fools of themselves in front of each other provided there was neither reprehension nor ridicule from the other. 'I've worked with far less famous actresses who behaved in a much, much more "starry" way than her,' he was able to say at the end of filming. 'She's fabulous, just fabulous.'

Nicole knew she would regret it for the rest of her life if she passed up on Satine. 'In terms of when I got the role I was absolutely floored,' she said. 'I was so excited. It was like a gift. And then the reality of playing it set in because when we got to Sydney it was like, OK, now we're going to do a read-through. But with a read-through on a musical you're not just reading lines, you've got to sing. And you've got to sing unaccompanied and you have to hope you're in the right key. It's very, very confronting. And it leaves you feeling very exposed. But that's what's brilliant about Baz. He actually pushes you early on so by the time you start to film you are comfortable with what you are doing, you are ready to try anything and do anything.'

As part of her preparation and partly out of curiosity, Nicole sat down to watch as many movie musicals from the past as she could. She emerged with enormous renewed respect for actresses such as Cyd Charisse, Rita Hayworth and, of course, Marilyn Monroe. They were all remarkably gifted, each in their own individual way, she decided, but Rita Hayworth was the one she especially singled out. 'I discovered Rita Hayworth whom I'd never appreciated as much as I did when I watched *Gilda* – and she's jaw-droppingly good. I've seen that film four or five times now. Each time I get blown away by her impact. So beautiful, so charismatic, an extraordinary dancer. She takes your breath away as a performer,' said Nicole.

Typically dedicated, Nicole practised her scales and learned to read music but was always mindful that Baz wanted her voice to come from her heart. Voice coach Andrew Ross was entrusted with the task of building on and exploiting what singing ability she and Ewan already had. Ross was adamant that *Moulin Rouge* should not suffer from what he called 'the Audrey Hepburn complex', when cinema audiences thought they were being cheated, that the voices had been tampered with or a voice double had been used. Baz was further insistent that Nicole and Ewan should be convincing enough, good enough and honest enough vocally to avoid audiences asking why they were singing at certain points in the story when they could just as well have been speaking their lines. Gradually the voices that suited them were allowed to evolve, culminating for Nicole in a sultry lounge singer's timbre.

Once Ewan and Nicole had been cast, a series of workshops ensued from July to November 1999, held at the renovated asylum which was the headquarters of Baz Luhrmann's Sydney company Bazmark. These consisted of music and dance lessons, improvisation and readings. Eventually, Nicole encouragingly found she could sing as Satine but not as Nicole.

It was intensive work during the day, but in the evening it was an opportunity for everyone to party, fully encouraged by Baz. The real Moulin Rouge in turn of the century Paris had been a decadent club where absinthe flowed unchecked, so one infamous high-spirited evening Baz served up the hallucinogenic green spirit favoured by bohemians of that era. Unsurprisingly, after that no one could remember much about the carousing that went on that particular evening.

Moulin Rouge was set to start shooting in late 1999 with a budget of $50 million but filming got off to the saddest of starts when Baz's father Leonard died of skin cancer. The director eventually dedicated *Moulin Rouge* to him but his death meant Baz starting a week behind schedule.

There were further unforeseen and unfortunate delays when Nicole broke a rib in rehearsal shortly before the cameras were due to start rolling. She maintains that her co-star has given her permission to say that it was he who was responsible so she says: 'We were doing the dance sequence where I had to jump into his arms. Neither of us is a trained dancer, and so it was just the way he caught me. It wasn't a full break, it was a small crack. But then they put me in a corset a little too soon and re-broke it.' Nicole's injury put the production even further behind schedule. It was a worry for everyone as the big new *Star Wars* movie was scheduled to move into the Sydney studios when *Moulin Rouge* was completed.

Cracked ribs were not the only serious injury Nicole suffered. Filming was in sight of completion when she tripped while wearing three-inch heels and fell awkwardly and very painfully down a flight of stairs. It was a huge shock for the actress. Her knee was badly injured. 'We were actually doing the "Diamonds Are a Girl's Best Friend" number which is at the beginning of the film,' she said. 'We had three days to shoot it and we had to work seventeen hours a day. At about one in the morning we were all really tired and we had to get the shot. I said: "Yeah, yeah, we'll just do one more take." I replay that moment in my head, because I was in these huge heels and I just fell down the stairs and tore the cartilage behind my kneecap.' Painkillers and a determination that the show must go on pulled Nicole through and bravely she shot her final close-ups on crutches. Her knee eventually required surgery.

Unfortunate mishaps notwithstanding, *Moulin Rouge* was driven along by Baz Luhrmann with his customary unrelenting enthusiasm and unshakeable belief that it was possible to achieve absolutely anything. Although he was, of course, at the helm, Baz saw re-creating Paris in a Sydney studio as a team project and gathered everyone together before shooting began to give them all a pep talk.

With Baz, the movie was constantly evolving and changing. It was a spontaneous way of working which, for the most part, was inspiring, but could prove occasionally galling for some when something assiduously rehearsed was suddenly changed. Almost always, however, the change was for the better, cast and crew had to admit as they watched Baz's wide-ranging ambition bear fruit.

While visiting India in 1994 to research an opera based on *A Midsummer Night's Dream*, Baz took in a Bollywood movie. 'It was corny comedy, incredible drama and then suddenly a musical number,' he recalls. 'Everyone was riveted. Could it work with an audience in the West?' *Moulin Rouge* was his chance to find out, and Baz let his fertile imagination take flight. He envisioned a spectacular musical the like of which the cinema would never have seen before, an extravaganza of period drama, modern music and lavish beyond all expectation. With filming stretched over six sound stages, the sheer scale of his ambition knew no bounds. He was willing to try anything. For the big production numbers, up to 500 performers were on camera at any one time; up to 400 extras, all elaborately costumed and choreographed, were required for some scenes; there were dancers galore, acrobats, a giant elephant statue and, of course, a red windmill. His extraordinary psychedelic vision for a Bombay musical scene employed ten different dance styles, incredible costumes, a techno beat and 100 top hats flung joyously into the air simultaneously.

For Satine, Baz had in mind elements of Madonna, Monroe and Marlene Dietrich. For Nicole, the appeal of playing Satine included the fun of dressing up and the chance to be extravagant with her performance, her clothes and the way she moved. There were also funny, mad moments to savour – notably the occasion when as Satine she is perched high up on a trapeze with 600 male extras arrayed below her awaiting Baz's shouted direction: 'Unbridled lust! Unbridled lust! Show us unbridled lust!'

Baz described his approach to *Moulin Rouge* as a Red Curtain theatre style. 'We take a simple story based on a primary myth and set it in a heightened, created world that is at once exotic yet also recognisable,' he explained.

But he never lost sight of the fact that in the middle of his exotic mix was the story of the love between Satine and Christian and he wanted truthfulness for that love story. Although used to being a courtesan, Satine also longs to escape that world and is suddenly caught unaware by Christian whose belief in love conquering all utterly captivates her.

At the heart of *Moulin Rouge* is the sizzling Satine, the sparkling diamond of the Moulin Rouge and the most famous courtesan in Paris. Ewan McGregor is Christian, the idealistic young poet who comes to the French capital in search of love, but who leaves his respectable life to enter the Montmartre underworld and, in particular, the decadent world of the Moulin Rouge. There he meets the artist Toulouse-Lautrec (John Leguizamo) and Zidler (Jim Broadbent), owner of the Moulin Rouge, the nightclub of the century where anything goes – except falling in love. Soon Satine finds herself caught between the love and devotion of Christian and the obsession of the Duke (Richard Roxburgh), a wealthy aristocrat who is able to offer her legitimate stardom.

As the central character of Satine, Nicole worked seven days a week for eight months. She averaged only about five hours of sleep a night, regularly working sixteen-hour days, sometimes supervising her children's homework in between takes. Just being made-up could take three hours each day and it took up to twenty minutes for her to be laced into a corset. Weekends brought no respite because there was recording to be done on Saturdays and Sundays as well as rehearsing, learning rewrites and new choreography. She would often start her day at five and still be in the recording studio in the small hours of the following morning.

Perhaps the trickiest song for Nicole to tackle was 'Diamonds Are a Girl's Best Friend'. It was so quintessentially Marilyn Monroe's, so distinctive, that Nicole tried it several ways before coming up with a more raunchy vocal from the chest rather than Marilyn's breathy, twee, coquettish delivery.

Nicole said she developed a 'deep emotional admiration' for co-star Ewan. 'I found it much easier to play the love on screen through song because it extends the emotion,' she explained. 'It lets you get lost in it, particularly when Ewan sang Elton John's 'Your Song'. I must have heard it 600 times but every time he did it, it still evoked an immediate emotional adoration of him.'

After almost 200 days of dedicated, sometimes frenzied, endeavour, shooting finally finished on *Moulin Rouge* and there was much excitement among cast and crew when they learned that the movie would open the 54th Cannes Film Festival on 9 May 2001.

Unveiling a movie with a uniquely Parisian flavour to the French, in their own country, as a curtain raiser for probably the world's most prestigious film festival, might have been asking for a slap in the face. But one thing was certain – the movie was not going to lack Nicole Kidman's promotional support.

It would have been understandable if she had fought shy of interviews and backed out of personal appearances having featured recently in so many headlines about the break-up of her marriage and the loss of her baby. But Nicole had put too much into *Moulin Rouge* to let the film hit the screens without her full backing. And she was proud of it. 'I believe in this film and I really loved working with Baz,' she said. 'I saw him practically kill himself for this movie and I'm going to be right there for him.' Nicole was nervous about meeting a voracious, inquisitive media at Cannes but she was grateful it was at least to discuss a movie she believed in and was excited about and could genuinely enthuse over. She knew there would still be intense interest in her personal life – but she also understood that would be the case.

'I'm so glad I've made a love story,' she told one interviewer. 'The message of the film is that no matter what your experience, no matter what your path, no matter what goes on in your life, you can still fall in love. There's always hope of falling in love and stay open to it even if you maybe know it's not going to end the way you hoped.

'I'm still a great believer and a romantic. I suppose I believe in destiny and I believe there is a soulmate out there for every one of us. I'm determined to keep believing that.' She added poignantly: 'I love the message of the film which is that it's better to have loved and lost than never to have loved at all.'

There was no sign of Nicole wavering when she walked up the red carpet at the Palais des Festivals in Cannes on 9 May in front of a cheering crowd of onlookers. She may have been churning inside but she was poise itself, wearing a black strapless dress with a split ruffled skirt in keeping with the theme of *Moulin Rouge*. Her presence and her can-can style dress were boldly stating her loyalty to Baz and to the film. 'We still love you,' shouted a man in the crowd encouragingly, which brought a smile to Nicole's face.

Moulin Rouge was given its first screening to an audience of 2000, mainly French dignitaries, film-makers and actors, and to the joy and relief of all connected with the picture it received a thunderous eight-minute standing ovation. The critics, however, were divided. They seemed either to love or to hate *Moulin Rouge*. With its brash and brazen bravura, its colourfully costumed, crazy explosion of opera, dazzling dance and high camp, its slick editing, and sexy spectacle, it was hardly the kind of movie about which critics could sit on the fence. At one of the test screenings in America, one youthful member of the audience had ventured the opinion that it was *The Rocky Horror Picture Show* meets *Titanic*. Baz felt that was not such a bad summary of the film. 'It's set in a world heading towards tragedy, it's impossible love, it's an all-singing, all-dancing *Titanic*,' he laughed.

The Cannes Film Festival's opening-night party, usually a black tie affair, was this time tailored to the prize exhibit for the select guests and can-can girls. A large portion of the French resort was fenced off and giant circus marquees were erected alongside the harbour. Inside stood a huge windmill with glowing lights. Renowned disc jockey Fat Boy Slim was at the decks playing music designed to steam up the dance floor. At one point Nicole could be seen in the DJ's booth selecting records and then taking to the dance floor. Nothing was going to stop her enjoying her big night.

Nicole's performance in *Moulin Rouge*, as well as the way she coped with the personal trauma that had befallen her just as the film was gearing up for release, earned her unstinting admiration from Baz Luhrmann. He predicted audiences would love her as Satine and that they would discover in the film how incredibly funny she is. 'She's a comedienne, really whacky,' he said. As for her fortitude over her marriage break-up, he said: 'I don't think she's been crushed by it. I think she grows from it, and no one embodies the spirit of "the show must go on" more than Nicole.'

Baz pointed out that the Orphean myth underlying *Moulin Rouge* is about that moment in life when you realise that there are some things bigger than yourself. 'Some people will die, some relationships cannot be, no matter how perfect they are,' he said. 'And the idea of that myth is that you don't get crushed by it, that you grow from it.'

On 2 January 2002 after a string of rave reviews and a Best Actress Oscar nomination for *Moulin Rouge*, Nicole won the Best Actress award at the Golden Globes. As she stood up to accept it, warmly applauded by the Hollywood foreign press who host the event every year, she was by far the hottest actress in the world. Her other big movie of 2001, *The Others*, had topped $100 million at the box office.

Recently very publicly divorced, Nicole Kidman was the leading lady in two of the most commercially successful films of the year, and the irony was not lost on her. 'In a weird way, the best of times and the worst of times always come together,' she said, managing a smile as she accepted her award in front of many millions of TV viewers in dozens of countries around the world. They included Australia, which had a big night. As well as Nicole's gong, Russell Crowe won Best Actor for *A Beautiful Mind* and Baz Luhrmann picked up the award for Best Picture, Musical and Comedy for *Moulin Rouge*.

In Nicole's gracious speech there was, however, a dig at Tom Cruise, which was so devoid of blatant vitriol that it lost her no respect, and there was also a hint to suggest the famous Kidman spirit was anything but crushed. 'I want to thank all the people who have stuck by me,' said Nicole, who was accompanied to the ceremony by her mother and father. 'I have a number of people in my life who have been extraordinary – my elegant mama, my father who has such integrity, my sister who envelops me with warmth every day, and my two babies, who are very tolerant of their mother and I love them more than anything in the world.'

After winning the Golden Globe Best Actress award, Nicole was the early front-runner for the Oscars to be held on 24 March 2002. She was desperate to win, not least for Baz Luhrmann for showing such faith in her. But in the final run-up to the event it was apparent that the case for either Halle Berry for *Monster's Ball* or Judi Dench for *Iris* was gathering pace and that she would face stiff competition.

While her Best Actress rivals were able to beat the Hollywood drum in the weeks preceding the Oscars, Nicole was closeted in a hotel near the Swedish town of Trollhattan near Gothenburg working on *Dogville*, a low-budget movie directed by Lars von Trier. The maverick Danish director, who began his career in the 1970s with such cult classics as *The Elements of Crime* and *Europa*, had won the Cannes Palme d'Or in 2000 for *Dancer in the Dark* starring Icelandic singer Bjork. Now he had written a movie, set in the 1930s, specifically with Nicole in mind. His story centred on a woman who has grown up in a gangster family and who goes on the run and takes refuge in a small town populated by eccentrics.

When Nicole flew from the snows of Sweden to Los Angeles for the Oscars, there was much speculation as to who would be her date for the big night, particularly as Tom Cruise was certain to attend. He had been asked to open proceedings with a welcoming speech. In the event, Nicole chose to be accompanied by her sister Antonia and Nicole and Tom's paths did not cross.

Disappointingly for Nicole, she was pipped to the Oscar by Halle Berry. But although the big prize had eluded her, she was many people's choice as the most stylishly dressed actress at the ceremony. Nicole shimmered in a delicately romantic pale-pink chiffon Chanel dress topped off by a $4 million Bulgari 241-carat, rough-diamond necklace.

The Best Actress Oscar would have crowned a momentous year for Nicole, but her disappointment at missing out was tempered by the announcement that she had been chosen to star in a new multi-million dollar movie called *Court and Spark* in which she would play Eleanor of Aquitaine, wife of English king Henry II and mother of Richard the Lionheart.

The plan was for the film to recreate the splendours of England's twelfth-century royal court, and scriptwriter Alan Howard summed up the scope of the role for Nicole by explaining, 'Eleanor has the civilising influence of Jacqueline Kennedy and the political skills of Eleanor Roosevelt and Margaret Thatcher. The movie will use this passionate and explosive love story of Eleanor and Henry to focus on this extraordinary life.'

Born the daughter of William, Duke of Aquitaine, in 1122, Eleanor was one of the richest women in Europe. She married Louis VII of France but began an affair with Henry, then Duke of Normandy. Her marriage was annulled by the Pope and she married Henry in 1152, becoming queen two years later.

Executives at the Fox Searchlight studio believed that Nicole could portray Eleanor's combination of beauty, grace and ruthlessness that historians and medieval chroniclers have described.

It was Nicole's great idol Katharine Hepburn who had previously played Eleanor on the big screen opposite Peter O'Toole as Henry II in the 1968 film *The Lion in Winter*. It was a role which Nicole was looking forward to with relish but, as she prepared to return to Sweden, she was able to say: 'If I live to 85, on my death bed I want to say I didn't just act or live or travel the world, I worked with some great directors, I was a great cook and a great mother.'

CHAPTER 15

Conclusion

'When you are in your thirties, you have taken some hits'
– NICOLE KIDMAN

'Hold your head high' was what Nicole Kidman's mother always used to say to her whenever her life hit a difficult patch. She listened to the advice when she was upset about being bullied at school and she listened to it again when her marriage collapsed in the most publicly painful manner imaginable. Now, just midway through her biblically allotted three score years and ten, for the shy Sydney schoolgirl turned internationally popular icon and award-winning actress, holding her head high is as important as it ever was.

' "Hold your head high" is what my mother always said,' recalls Nicole. 'No matter what happens, as long as you know you have conducted yourself properly, hold your head up.' No one could say that she had not conducted herself properly in the months since her marriage to Tom Cruise ended in a flurry of screaming headlines.

It is the strong and loving relationship that she has with her immediate family, followed by support from a group of long-standing close friends that has got Nicole Kidman through the nightmare of having her apparently idyllic world fall apart. She has devoted herself to her family and her first priority has been to protect her children from being harmed by the split. One of her great joys in life is lying in bed reading to her kids and seeing their faces light up. Nicole is a devoted mum. She tells her two adopted children: 'No, you didn't come from my tummy, but you came from my heart.'

Amazingly, she also managed to have a very good year professionally, surprising many people by her enormous strength in adversity. Not only did she attract phenomenal box office returns for *The Others* and *Moulin Rouge*, but she also reached the top of the pop charts with Robbie Williams.

Some actresses would have been horrified but when Robbie Williams rang to ask her to sing a duet of Frank and Nancy Sinatra's famous hit 'Somethin' Stupid', she said 'Why not?' Nicole thought Robbie had a wonderful voice and recording with him would be fun to do, which it was, with all the screaming publicity about the two stars locked in a sudden hot affair. It is not such a good story that the two were just good friends but it is the truth. Nicole loved the experience. And when a friend said the duet was wacky, Nicole responded: 'It's good that I'm wacky.'

Of course it could not compensate for her personal sadness and she hated the spotlight of publicity on her private life at such a terrible time. 'I've had the most intimate details of my life exposed in a way I never thought would happen,' said Nicole. But she has such a wonderful human support system in place and such remarkable strength of character that she can see benefits even in the personal disaster. 'I will look back on this time as surreal,' says Nicole. 'It's been horrible but at the same time it has allowed me freedom because I've gone, "OK. I'm dinner party gossip. I get looked at and talked about. That's humiliating but it doesn't get much worse than this and the kids are all right." ' Nicole says she never will discuss the details of the break-up with Tom but it will not be the end of her life. She will survive, as the song goes.

Nicole's parents Antony and Janelle are surely the key to the star's sanity. They keep her rooted in reality and she knows it. When Tom Cruise came to their home in William Edward Street, Longueville, Sydney to say he was in love with their daughter they were charmed but not dazzled. When the glittering marriage was over they were there for Nicole as she knew they would be. The qualities they value have nothing to do with celebrity or money and Nicole has them rooted deep within her.

That house she grew up in was a happy home. In fact her parents sold it only three years ago. Nicole chose a life that would lead her to travel all over the world in the sure knowledge that she has a loving family in Sydney to come home to if ever she needs them.

Whatever she does, she does with wholehearted enthusiasm. When she fell for Tom Cruise she did not hesitate. 'I was twenty-two years old and madly in love, following my heart and willing to throw caution to the wind,' she says. 'That is how I live my life. I'm spontaneous at times which can be dangerous. There are consequences but if you fall in love you fall in love. There is nothing you can do about that. If I had not followed through on that I would have denied myself and regretted it. I didn't care about the consequences – off I went. I left my apartment in Sydney and never went back. I called my sister and said, "You move in. I left all of my belongings." It is odd but the life of an actor is odd. Actors are odd. I come from a very stable background. My parents have lived in the same place for most of their lives. Only three years ago did they sell the house I grew up in so I would go back and stay in the bedroom that I grew up in with my daughter. So what seems normal to me is one place, one house and the same group of friends and it has taken me a long time to adjust to the gypsy lifestyle.'

Nicole also has six very close girlfriends on whom 'I could call at any time and who could call me, and we would be there for each other.' She is surprised that some people seem to think this is unusual. She feels: 'You have worked through stuff in your twenties, you have all lived some life. When you're in your thirties you have taken some hits. Some of my girlfriends are single mothers with kids, some have never been married, some are desperate to be married, some have been married twice. We've all had a substantial amount of life and now we're going, "You need your friends".'

She loves hard-working perfectionists and hates laziness. She flourishes with people who have energy and are totally involved and obsessed with what they are doing – like Stanley Kubrick, like Baz Luhrmann, like Sam Mendes, like Jane Campion. It was one of the great attractions too about Tom Cruise.

Nicole has tremendous energy and a huge thirst for knowledge and experience. She constantly tries to improve herself and further her knowledge. For instance, she took a poetry course in the Lake District where she visited Wordsworth's cottage and was able to go on walks and see the landscapes that inspired his poetry. Not content with loving Italy and visiting it as a tourist, she learned the language as well. She and Tom Cruise loved to holiday near Lucca.

Music is very important to Nicole. She says she could not live without it and has speakers all over the house. One of her favourite composers is Vivaldi. She once took Isabella to a church in Vienna for a concert of his music and her daughter whispered: 'Is it all right if I dance?' How could she refuse? So in this imposing church there was a cute little tot pirouetting in the aisle.

She also loves art and likes to collect black and white photographs – Steichen, Weston, Lee Miller or Man Ray. But when asked what painting she would like to live in she replied enigmatically: *The Scream* by Munch.

Just as her mother lightened Nicole's dark moments, she is determined to help her children through their fears and insecurities. She might look the most confident woman in the world but she still has to fight her own gremlins. When she was a girl she was frightened of getting on the bus for fear the boys would tease her and even today she feels trepidation before going into a crowded room. 'I get embarrassed but I try to throw that aside and beat it. Through my whole life I have tried to push through. It is so strange because I have chosen the worst career. But I don't run away from it. I push myself into it and make myself deal with it.'

Almost every other Hollywood star would have spent hours in therapy but Nicole, whose father is a psychologist, dares to be different. 'I haven't ever done therapy,' she smiles. 'Why do I act? I don't want to know. If you look at it, it is such a strange and ridiculous life. But I have an enormous respect for it and a lot of disgust, too. It's a complicated life but a wonderful life.'

In some ways her life has become more simple and clearly defined since the split from Tom Cruise. Now when she is asked about her religious beliefs she says: 'I'm not a Scientologist.'

The elegant slim figure of Nicole Kidman still seems the same as when she first burst on to the screen as a teenager. She is fortunate that she can eat anything she wants. She loves to run off any excess and used to do four miles a day until her accident on *Moulin Rouge*. In true Australian tradition she likes a drink from time to time and is something of a wine connoisseur.

Nicole has worked with some of the best actors and directors – Stanley Kubrick, Dustin Hoffman, John Malkovich, Gus Van Sant, Alec Baldwin, Jane Campion. Directors like working with her. 'Nicole is phenomenally modest and extremely accessible. She also has a great sense of humour,' says Joel Schumacher, who worked with her on *Batman Forever*. 'She was a really great ally on the set,' says Gus Van Sant, who directed her in *To Die For*. 'We never had disagreements. We just mostly had fun.'

Her range of roles has been wide. She has played a bereaved then terrorised mother in *Dead Calm*, a wilful gangster's moll in *Billy Bathgate*, a femme fatale in *Malice*, a skittish sex kitten in *Batman Forever*, the kindest, nicest, most caring woman imaginable in *My Life*, an abused wife in *The Portrait of a Lady*, a mail order bride in *The Birthday Girl*, and a consumptive can-can girl in *Moulin Rouge*.

But it has not always been easy. Being married to Tom Cruise can hinder as well as help a career and despite a solid body of good work, she doubted whether she would ever make it in mainstream American movies and had to go back to Australia and *Moulin Rouge* to make it really big. She had not become a member of that select group of Hollywood bankables until then. Now, thanks to *Moulin Rouge* and *The Others*, she is certainly a major Hollywood player. Even if she never wants to live in the place.

Nicole's public image has been enhanced by her dignified behaviour since the marriage split. She could have slunk away and hid. Instead she put herself out there promoting *Moulin Rouge* and *The Others*. She insisted on attending awards functions and appearing on TV without ducking the questions. Even when Michael Parkinson asked her bluntly about the split she was still frank and funny.

Back in her beloved high heels Nicole seems to have grown in stature and has won admiration from many. And the future looks busy and bright. One of her many unfulfilled ambitions is to write a novel. She knows it would take 'time and hibernation' but that is at least part of the attraction. She would also like to study philosophy and become more fluent in Italian. Ten years from now she hopes she is healthy and that her knee injury has healed enough for her to resume running long distances. But mostly she hopes her family are all happy and healthy. She remains resolutely optimistic for the future. She might be halfway to seventy but she says: 'I still believe the glass is half full.'

Filmography

Films
Bush Christmas, 1983

In the mountains of New South Wales a family of Australian kids including Helen (Nicole Kidman) are heading homeward for the Christmas holidays. On the way they unwittingly provide the information which allows a band of thieves to steal their father's horses. Deciding to make amends on their own, the children head off into the Blue Mountains to track down the horse thieves, using Aboriginal survival skills to keep themselves alive and on the trail.

Director Henri Safran

BMX Bandits, 1984

PJ, Goose and Judy (Nicole Kidman) are three Sydney teenagers enjoying the craze for riding their own BMX bikes when they stumble across a case of walkie-talkies desperately needed by a gang of crooks, led by the Boss (Bryan Marshall), for their next big job. When they test them out, they accidentally alert the police on the same waveband and find themselves chased by the gang of villains, the cops and an army of young BMX cyclists who ride to their rescue.

Director Brian Trenchard-Smith

Archer's Adventure, 1985

Action adventure movie starring Nicole Kidman and Robert Coleby in a tale about a trainer's apprentice volunteering to deliver an untested racehorse across 600 miles of rough terrain to take part in Australia's biggest horserace.

Director Denny Lawrence

Wills & Burke, 1985

Dry comedy based around the 1860 expedition by Robert Burke (Garry McDonald) and William Wills (Kim Gyngell) who set out with a team of camels on the first journey of exploration across the Australian continent. Their exploits during their trek across Australia are turned into a musical starring Julia Matthews (Nicole Kidman), the singer with whom Burke is obsessed.

Director Bob Weis

Windrider, 1986

PC Simpson (Tom Burlinson) is the fast-talking, wise-cracking son of the boss of a wealthy Australian engineering firm. He is witty and irreverent and, although he works for his father's firm, his great passion in life is windsurfing. He enlists the company's engineer to help develop a high-tech windsurfing board. Then he meets Jade Kelly (Nicole Kidman), the stunning lead singer of an up-and-coming rock band, who is motivated, eager, energetic and extremely ambitious. Their worlds are poles apart, but they fall in love, lose each other, and are reunited in time for Jade to give PC her love and support as he challenges his deadly rival Coyote in the world windsurfing championships.

Director Vincent Monton

Nightmaster, 1987

A class of gifted pupils, including Nicole Kidman, at a prep school are strictly controlled by day, but at night they are given martial arts lessons and take part in paintball wargames organised by a sadistic teacher Mr Beck. Gradually he exerts an increasing amount of control over the lives of the pupils who are unaware that the games are a cover for a drug ring.

Director Mark Joffe

Emerald City, 1989

Comedy, based on a play by David Williamson, about Australian screenwriter Colin Rogers (John Hargreaves) who gives up the rural life to move with his wife Kate (Robyn Nevin), who works in publishing, to Sydney and the high life. Joining the Sydney social whirl, Colin gets mixed up with Mike McCord (Chris Haywood), a small-time movie man who believes in more money and less integrity in the world of film-making. Colin also meets Mike's very sexy young girlfriend Helen (Nicole Kidman), who makes it plain she fancies Colin. Dazzled by Helen, Colin almost embarks on an affair with her while Kate is also scheming to have an affair of her own. Also starring Ruth Cracknell.

Director Michael Jenkins

Dead Calm, 1989

Happily married couple John and Rae Ingram (Sam Neill and Nicole Kidman) find peace alone on the Pacific on their well-equipped yacht after the trauma of the death of their baby son in a car accident. But their tranquillity is nightmarishly transformed when they come to the aid of a lone yachtsman Hughie (Billy Zane) who has abandoned a sinking schooner on which, he says, all other passengers and crew have died from food poisoning. Leaving Hughie asleep, John goes across to the dilapidated vessel only to discover dead bodies in the bilges and a video indicating a deranged Hughie killed all on board. While he is away, Hughie overpowers Rae and sets off in the opposite direction. For Rae, it is the start of a terrifying cat-and-mouse game with the vicious young killer and a race against time to save her husband.

Director Phillip Noyce

Flirting, 1989

Danny Embling (Noah Taylor) is a picked-on teenage schoolboy whose parents have sent him in 1965 to a strict, boys-only, rural boarding school across the lake from a similar educational establishment for girls. Relief from peer pressure comes from Thandiwe (Thandie Newton), a young Uganda student from the girls' school who is the daughter of an African nationalist lecturer. When Danny meets Thandiwe, who is suffering racial slurs, they are immediately attracted to each other and become kindred spirits, lovers and problems for their teachers. The only support the couple receive is from Nicola Radcliffe (Nicole Kidman), a head prefect who is outwardly disapproving but inwardly sympathetic to their plight.

Director John Duigan

Days of Thunder, 1990

Genre film about stock car racing with Tom Cruise as cocky young up-and-coming driver Cole Trickle trying to break into the big time. Randy Quaid as Tim Daland, the owner of a used car dealership, persuades racing veteran Harry Hogge, played by Robert Duvall, to build him a competitive car providing that Trickle can race if for him. Trickle, aided by Hogge as his ruthless and duplicitous manager, tries to unseat Michael Rooker as Rowdy Burns, the experienced champion. But Trickle starts to reassess his life when both he and Burns end up in the same hospital where Trickle falls for Dr Claire Lewicki (Nicole Kidman) who helps nurse him towards recovery.

Director Tony Scott

Billy Bathgate, 1991

Adaptation of E. L. Doctorow's novel about Dutch Schultz (Dustin Hoffman), gangster king of the 1930s New York underworld, who takes his once-trusted top enforcer (Bruce Willis) for a nocturnal ride in a tugboat, tying him up and planting his feet in cement before tipping him over the side to his death. But observing this murderous act at close quarters is Billy (Loren Dean), a streetwise kid who has worked his way up from the mean streets of the Bronx to become one of fiery mobster Dutch's treasured flunkies. As the Feds mercilessly move in on Dutch, Billy vows to take care of the beautiful Drew Preston (Nicole Kidman), the luckless dead enforcer's girlfriend. But by falling for the sultry, strong-willed Drew, he becomes ensnared in a dangerous love triangle that threatens to get them both killed.

Director Robert Benton

Far and Away, 1992

Tom Cruise stars as Joseph, the son of a poor Irish farmer in the 1890s out for vengeance for the death of his father and the burning of their home. When he falls for Shannon, the high-spirited daughter (Nicole Kidman) of his sworn enemy, he discovers she is as eager to escape her stuffy environment as he is to escape poverty. Together they travel to America posing as brother and sister where she works plucking chickens and he becomes a bare knuckle fighter. But as they join the rush for land in Oklahoma, they realise they are destined to cross the class divide and become lovers.

Director Ron Howard

Malice, 1993

College dean (Bill Pullman) is worried about the unknown rapist who has attacked several students in a sleepy New England college town. He is also worried about the mysterious abdominal pains his wife Tracy (Nicole Kidman) is suffering. Then into their lives steps a self-confident surgeon Jed (Alec

Baldwin) who is new to the area and moves into the third floor of the house. When he has to perform emergency surgery on Tracy, it sets off a twisting chain of chilling revelations. Also featuring Anne Bancroft.

Director Harold Becker

My Life, 1993

Bob Jones (Michael Keaton) is confronting terminal cancer and prepares a videotape about himself for the yet to be born child his wife (Nicole Kidman) is carrying. She gently cajoles him into seeing a healer and at the healing sessions he reveals himself to bear a seething hostility against his father and much darker emotions besides.

Director Bruce Joel Rubin

Batman Forever, 1995

The second *Batman* sequel with Val Kilmer donning the Dark Knight's cape to do battle with Two-Face (Tommy Lee Jones), a one-time district attorney turned bad after having his face scarred by acid, who is terrorising Gotham. Along the way Batman encounters Dr Chase Meridian (Nicole Kidman), a criminal psychologist who sets her romantic sights on Gotham's hero. With Chris O'Donnell and Jim Carrey as the villainous Riddler.

Director Joel Schumacher

To Die For, 1995

Black comedy based on the book by Joyce Maynard about Suzanne Stone (Nicole Kidman), a young woman in a small town called Little Hope, who lives to be on TV. Her brazen ambition helps her to force her way into a job on her local cable TV station as a weather girl. But once she has had a taste of local TV, her dream of becoming a famous national TV personality becomes a nightmare as ambition turns to obsession. She determines to conquer the world of television and will stop at nothing to get ahead, including persuading her teenage lover (Joaquin Phoenix) to kill her husband Larry (Matt Dillon), who threatens to stand in the way of her thrust for TV fame.

Director Gus Van Sant

The Leading Man, 1996

Guest appearance from Nicole Kidman playing herself at an awards ceremony in a film about infidelity set in London's theatre world. Starring Jon Bon Jovi, Anna Galiena and Thandie Newton.

Director John Duigan

The Portrait of a Lady, 1996

The study of a nineteenth-century woman trapped in the mores of her time, based on the Henry James story. Isabel Archer (Nicole Kidman) is a single-minded American heiress in Europe who turns down proposals of marriage from both her American and British suitors (Viggo Mortensen and Richard E. Grant) because she wants to explore life. But in Italy the apparently friendly Madame Merle (Barbara Hershey) steers her into a loveless match with manipulating, penniless, cruel and controlling artist Gilbert Osmond (John Malkovich). Also featuring John Gielgud, Shelley Winters and Shelley Duvall.

Director Jane Campion

The Peacemaker, 1997

Dr Julia Kelly (Nicole Kidman), acting head of the White House Nuclear Smuggling Group, teams up with Lt Col Tom Devoe (George Clooney), an intelligence officer with Army Special Forces, after nuclear bombs are stolen from a Russian train carrying them to be defused. The train has been wrecked in a crash to make it look as though all the bombs were destroyed, but Devoe sees through the ruse and a hunt begins for a terrorist with a grudge against the US who is planning to explode one of the bombs in Manhattan.

Director Mimi Leder

Practical Magic, 1998

Sally Owens (Sandra Bullock) and her sister Gillian (Nicole Kidman) were raised by their aunts following the death of their parents. Once grown up they go their separate ways, Sally enjoying a quiet life while Gillian freewheels from town to town and from man to man. When Gillian's latest relationship turns sour, Sally comes to the rescue and releases dark forces that threaten to destroy their family.

Director Griffin Dunne

Eyes Wide Shut, 1999

Based on a short novel by the Viennese playwright and physician Arthur Schnitzler, *Traumnovelle*, this powerful story of sexual jealousy tells the story of Dr William Harford (Tom

Cruise) and his wife Alice (Nicole Kidman) whose happy life together spirals into danger after a drug-fuelled row during which she confesses to fantasising about a handsome sea captain they once met. The wealthy couple are subsequently driven apart during a night of erotic adventure – and a day of reckoning.

Director Stanley Kubrick

Moulin Rouge, 2001

A poet (Ewan McGregor) defies his father by moving to the Montmartre district of Paris, France. There he finds himself swept up into the Bohemian world of Toulouse-Lautrec and his entourage and is recruited to write a nightclub spectacular. In this seedy world of sex and drugs, he embarks on a passionate affair with the club's highest paid star and courtesan Satine (Nicole Kidman). With Jim Broadbent, John Leguizamo, Richard Roxburgh and Kylie Minogue.

Director Baz Luhrmann

The Others, 2001

Chilling tale of psychological terror set on the secluded island of Jersey in the final days of the Second World War, where Grace (Nicole Kidman) waits for her beloved husband (Christopher Eccleston) to return from the front. Grace has been raising their two young children alone in a beautiful, cavernous Victorian mansion, the one place she believes them to be safe. But when three new servants arrive to replace the ones who inexplicably disappeared, startling supernatural events begin to unfold. At first Grace is unwilling to believe in her children's frightening sightings, but soon she too begins to sense that intruders are at large. With Fionnula Flanagan, Eric Sykes and Elaine Cassidy.

Director Alejandro Amenabar

Birthday Girl, 2002

John Buckingham (Ben Chaplin), an English bank manager, orders a Russian bride called Nadia (Nicole Kidman) from an on-line mail order service called From Russia With Love. He's requested a bride he can talk to, but Nadia arrives knowing only one word of English – yes. He soon finds his life turned upside down with the arrival of two of her Russian cousins who take her hostage and force the new husband to rob his own bank.

Director Jez Butterworth

The Hours, 2002

The story of three women in different places and different time periods of the twentieth century who are trying to define their identity in a world that wants them to behave differently. They are Virginia Woof (Nicole Kidman), who is depicted working on a novel as she recovers from depression in 1923; Julianne Moore is a Los Angeles housewife who reads Woolf's novel in 1949 as she organises a party for her husband; Meryl Streep is a 1990s woman in New York planning a farewell party for her former lover.

Director Stephen Daldry

Dogville, 2002

Set in an American mountain village in the 1930s, Nicole Kidman plays Grace, a woman who has grown up in a gangster family, who goes on the run and takes refuge in a small town populated by eccentrics. Also starring Lauren Bacall, Chloe Sevigny and Katrin Cartlidge.

Director Lars Von Trier

Major Television Roles
Chase Thru the Night, 1986

Mini-series based on a tense story by Australian writer Max Fatchen about a remote country town being taken over by three fleeing bank robbers. Nicole played young Petra, who was taken hostage by the villains. Also starring John Jarratt.

Winners, 1986

Children's TV series focusing on social issues affecting young people. In episode six, Nicole played schoolgirl Carol, a dedicated 1500-metre runner coached by an enthusiastic father. But at school she befriends a new pupil called Angie, a punk with aspirations to dance. Carol has always longed to be able to dance and, much to the annoyance of her parents, breaks off from her athletics training regime to attend dance classes. On the day of the Combined Sports Carnival, Carol comes only second in the 1500 metres but has proved to herself there are more goals in life than one.

A Country Practice, 1984

Two episodes as glue-sniffing teenager Simone Jenkins in the long-running TV series about a small medical practice in fictional Wandin Valley in rural New South Wales.

Five Mile Creek, 1984

Guest role as tough teenager Annie in adventure series about Five Mile Creek, an isolated coach stop run by two women on a stage line between the harbour town of Port Nelson and the mining camp of Wilga in Australia at the time of the 1860s gold rush.

Vietnam, 1986

Powerful drama serial exploring Australia's controversial involvement in the Vietnam War. Nicole Kidman starred as an awkward fourteen-year-old schoolgirl who grows up into an outspoken and free-thinking twenty-four-year-old anti-war protester and campaigner.

An Australian in Rome, 1986

An Italian matriarch interferes with a love triangle which develops between her two sons and a naïve Australian tourist called Jill (Nicole Kidman) who is visiting the sights in Rome.

The Bit Part, 1989

Nicole starred as aspiring actress Mary McAllister in a TV movie about Mike Thornton, a school careers counsellor who quits his boring job to become an actor. Unfortunately he discovers that acting is a job filled with inconvenient things like auditions and having to accept lowly small roles just to pay the bills. But he does manage to have a fling with Mary until she realises life might be more interesting in Hollywood and promptly leaves.

Bangkok Hilton, 1989

Powerful drama with Nicole Kidman as Kat Stanton, a shy young Australian girl searching for her missing father, who winds up in the infamous Thai prison known as the Bangkok Hilton facing the death sentence after her evil drug dealer boyfriend tricks her into smuggling for him. Co-starring Denholm Elliott as Kat's father, the searing thriller, specially written for Nicole, was inspired by a shocking real-life incident of an Irish terrorist who sent his pregnant girlfriend to her death by putting a bomb in her luggage on a flight.

Sources

T he authors have respected the wishes of many interview subjects to remain anonymous and accordingly they are not mentioned in the book. They gratefully acknowledge the following sources who helped in the preparation of this book but they are by no means all-inclusive:

The Age, Australian TV Week, Woman's Day, Daily Telegraph, Mirror, Sunday Telegraph, Australian Rolling Stone, McCall's Magazine, Daily Mirror, Juice Magazine, Talk Magazine, Newsweek, The Australian, Vanity Fair, Sunday Times, Sunday Mail (Brisbane), *Geelong Advertiser, Australian Woman, Sydney Morning Herald, Australian Women's Weekly, Movieline Magazine, Redbook, Los Angeles*

Times, Brisbane Courier Mail, TV Week, Marie Claire, Melbourne Herald-Sun, Elle, New Idea, Cosmopolitan, Woman's Own, 60 Minutes, Now Magazine, Ladies' Home Journal, Vogue, Entertainment Weekly, Us Magazine.

Index